My Life, A Little Off-Balance

My Life, A Little Off-Balance

What I've Learned about Jesus, Joy, and Life with Cerebral Palsy

Amelia McNeilly

with Jeanne Harrison

DEDICATION

To Donnie and Sara

"My parents are my best friends. I am thankful to the Lord every day that He chose them to be mine. Each day they represent Jesus to me, and I will never be able to thank them enough for how they have blessed me. They are my heroes!"

-excerpt from Amelia's blog

CONTENTS

FOREWORD

I met Amelia almost ten years ago, shortly after she became the booking agent for a comic that brought me on the road as an opener. We first met in Los Angeles, at the home of the headlining comedian. We chatted for a little bit and then Amelia said she had to go get something from the guest room. She stood up, began walking, and then fell flat on the floor. I moved to help her, but she'd already bounced back up, continuing on toward the room. She was completely un-phased.

"Um, are you okay?" I asked, unsure of what to do.

"Yeah, I just have some balance issues," she said casually. "It happens all the time."

And it did. But Amelia always bounced back up, undaunted.

Amelia was the friend God knew I needed. I was a closed off, introverted, and socially awkward new comic. None of this phased Amelia and she acted like we'd been friends our entire lives. A few weeks after our first meeting, she called to confirm some booking details and said, "I'm so glad to have such a good friend like you, Kristin!"

"Am I a good friend?" I thought. "We barely know each other!"

I was not a good friend. Amelia, however, was an incredible friend and taught me a lot about friendship. She cared deeply for souls and made each person she encountered feel important. She was legitimately interested in how you were doing, which stood out because in Hollywood most people only express interest in someone if that person can help their career in some way.

Amelia called fairly often to discuss various comedy show details, but she always ended each conversation by asking her trademark question, "How can I be praying for you?"

At first, I'd simply answer, "pray I have wisdom," because I never can think of prayer requests on the spot. (And who can't use more wisdom in their life?) I think Amelia caught on, though, because she began asking follow-up questions about my life. About comedy. About my faith. Then, she'd say she would be praying for those things.

Over time, Amelia and I bonded over our mutual love of books and theology and quirky comedies. I began looking forward to our conversations and, when we could manage it, actual visits. I even began writing down prayer requests, so I'd remember them when she asked.

When Amelia said she was praying for you, you knew without a doubt she was approaching the throne of God on your behalf. Even toward the end of her life, when the hospital bed in her room became her full-time mission field, she never stopped praying for others.

A few months before she went to be home with Jesus, Amelia and I were talking on the phone. She told me that she had to go because some people had come over to say hello and check on her. I knew the truth, though. People came over to be ministered to by Amelia. "Checking in on her" was merely a cover. You left her company filled up. Her physical limitations were simply used by God to get people to her bedside so they could be healed by His message of hope.

Amelia's faith never wavered, despite her CP and its physical complications. She completely trusted God's faithfulness and goodness. Her love for the Lord was both infectious and inspiring. A couple months after her death, I went to visit Sara and Donnie and they gave me a Bible that had belonged to Amelia. As I flipped through the Psalms, I stopped at a passage in Psalm 27 that she'd underlined: "I am still confident of this: I will see the goodness of the Lord in the land of the living. Wait for the Lord, be strong and take heart, and wait for the Lord" (Psalm 27:13-14).

Amelia knew Jesus in a unique and special way here on earth, and now she's fully alive in the presence of her Lord, no longer waiting, but seeing the promise she so faithfully put her hope in while on earth.

Kristin Weber
Author and Comedian

INTRODUCTION

Whenever I think about Amelia, I think of my husband's shiny Acura TL. It was a beautiful car—silver with a black leather interior. Amelia called it "the bat mobile," and it was responsible for bringing us together in the first place. The year was 2004 and we were both enrolled at Columbia International University, a small Bible college in South Carolina.

Every student was required to take a field education class, volunteering in various placements around the community. Amelia and I both chose the local crisis pregnancy center. On the first day of class, she sat beside me. "Hey! I saw we both signed up for the same placement. Want to carpool?" We barely knew each other, but Amelia was disarmingly sweet. She was petite, with short curly hair, arm crutches, and a radiant smile.

"Sure!" I said. "Do you have a car?"

"Nope. I was hoping you did."

Later I mentioned the dilemma to my boyfriend, Clint, casually eyeing his TL, which was easily the most expensive car on campus. He smiled, "Of course you can take my car."

The first time I pulled up in front of Amelia's dorm, she was duly impressed. "Hop in!" I grinned.

"That's not a car. That's a bat mobile!" Amelia laughed. It was true; the moment the doors shut it felt other-worldly—dark, black, and quiet. Once a week we cruised around town in the bat mobile, talking about life, college, and the girls at the pregnancy center. I loved that time with her.

After undergrad we went our separate ways. Clint and I got married. We traded in the bat mobile for a baby and a responsible Honda Civic. Amelia accepted an internship that launched her career. It was the dawn of the social media age, and occasionally we caught glimpses of one another's lives in isolated snapshots.

Then one day, twelve years later, Amelia reached out to me for help with a project. She wanted to blog for thirty-one days straight about a single topic, but she didn't have the stamina to do it alone. Would I like to contribute a post? "Of course!" I replied. "Tell me more about the project. Tell me how you are!" That was when I learned two things. Amelia had just qualified for hospice care, and the topic she wanted to blog about was gratitude.

To say I was stunned is an understatement. For all our time riding around in the bat mobile, we'd never had a very deep relationship. I didn't ask about her disability because I didn't want to make her uncomfortable. But now she was dying, and I wanted very much to know everything. *How do you feel? What can I do? Why is this happening?*

We began having a weekly phone date. This time, no holds barred. We were twelve years older, wiser, and more battle-scarred by life. I asked her all kinds of questions, often prefacing them with, "You don't have to answer this if you don't want to."

She always answered.

She loved letting me into her life, and she made me an extravagant offer. "Let me pray for you. I mean it, Jeanne. Anytime. I'm completely bed bound; I have all the time in the world to pray.

Just shoot me a text when you really need prayer, and I'll pray right then."

It's an incredible thing to have access to that kind of support. I never worried about how Amelia viewed me or what she thought of me. I just opened my heart to her. I texted her things I didn't share with anyone else—quick cries for prayer in dark moments. And she was always there. Even when she was asleep, or unable to respond for days because of her health, I knew she was there.

To this day, I still ponder why exactly Amelia and I connected so deeply the second time around. Maybe it was the fact that I was in a tough season of transition and desperately needed a godly friend. Maybe it was the fact that she was dying and there was no time to waste. Or maybe it was simply because of Amelia's nature. Despite the numerous friends she had, she made each one believe they were her favorite. Whatever the case may be, in the final months of her life, Amelia climbed inside my heart and became an ever-present voice in my head.

During one of our early phone dates, Amelia talked about her desire to compile her blogs into a book about her life. She had plenty of passion, but not enough energy to do it alone. Meanwhile, for months I had been asking God to direct me to my next writing project. It didn't take a rocket scientist to connect the dots! We talked excitedly about the book for a while—making all kinds of plans—until it became clear that Amelia was much weaker than she had let on. Without really acknowledging anything, we set the project aside and just enjoyed one another. When Amelia passed away on July 9,

2018, her mom reached out to me again. This time, we were determined to see Amelia's legacy in print.

Before she died, Amelia contributed several thoughts to this book, starting with the title. She picked it a long time ago, since thanks to CP, she has learned to live life a little off-balance from the day she was born. To me, the title is beautiful on so many levels. Not only did Amelia physically live a little off-balance, but in her humility, she recognized that spiritually we are all a little off-balance. Like awkward toddlers, we need the strong arms of our Father God to catch us when we fall, guide us in His ways, and hold our hands until the day we see Him face to face.

In addition to the title, Amelia and I decided to structure the book around one of her favorite quotes from the Christian pop duo, King and Country. In 2014 King and Country released a song called "Without you." The song was born out of one singer's battle with ulcerative colitis, which nearly claimed his life. It touched Amelia deeply, coinciding with some of her own major medical complications that forced her to become homebound. One line from the song became a theme for Amelia: "So let's dance a little, laugh a little, and hope a little more."

In the following pages, you will find Amelia's beautiful words, an overflow of her extraordinary heart. They are divided into three sections that capture her zest for life, her commitment to choose joy, and her unwavering focus on eternity. At the start of each section, I've written a little bit about Amelia's life based on conversations we had and correspondence with her mother. If she were still alive, I know it would be Amelia's prayer that as you read her book you encounter Jesus, welcome Him into your life, and in so doing, learn to dance a little, laugh a little, and hope a little more in Him.

DANCE A LITTLE MORE

"Courage, dear heart."

~*C.S. Lewis*

HOW AMELIA DANCED

Placental Abruption. To Donnie and Sara McNeilly the words simply translated: bedrest, and lots of it. Because their baby's placenta had detached from the womb, Sara would need to take it extra easy as she carried their precious cargo. So she did. For months Sara remained in bed, eagerly awaiting the arrival of their little girl. Then one day, at twenty-eight weeks pregnant, her body went into labor. Because of the placental abruption and the fact that she was twelve weeks early, she was put in an ambulance and rushed from her small town of Casar, North Carolina, to Charlotte. By the time she arrived in Charlotte, Sara was bleeding profusely. "We're not concerned about saving the baby," doctors told her. "We're concerned about saving your life."

Little did they know, Someone Else was incredibly concerned about saving that baby. Against all odds, Amelia Ann McNeilly was born on January 9, 1985. She weighed just two pounds two ounces. In the years that have passed, turning vivid memories hazy, two things still stand out clearly to Amelia's mother: she was so beautiful and so strong. Even then. "We should've known what a fighter she was going to be," Sara muses. For three months Amelia fought for her life in the NICU of Carolina's HealthCare Hospital. And then one morning, shortly before taking her home, Donnie and Sara received fateful news. *Some bleeding on Amelia's brain...brain damage at birth or shortly after...*

Donnie remembers the doctors mentioning the possibility of cerebral palsy, but Sara doesn't remember it. "At the time it didn't seem like a big deal," she reflects. After all, Amelia was alive! So there was some bleeding on her brain; it was one detail in the midst of a remarkable birth story! But unbeknownst to them, the bleeding would dramatically impact Amelia's life.

When she was four pounds fifteen ounces, Donnie and Sara brought their baby home. "She was so tiny but so wonderful!" they remember. Right from the start, the three bonded deeply and profoundly. As her first year unfolded, Donnie and Sara knew Amelia was behind developmentally. At one year old, she could not sit unassisted nor crawl. But then again, she scarcely weighed twelve pounds! When her pediatrician urged them to have her evaluated, Sara recalls that she wasn't upset because she assumed Amelia would catch up eventually. "The joy of being young and dumb!" She quips.

They went to the Developmental Evaluation Center on April 1, 1986. Sara remembers it like it was yesterday. "I had on a floral skirt and tan sweater and Amelia had on pink overalls and white tennis shoes." After putting Amelia through a series of tests, doctors delivered the results. "They called us into a room and told us Amelia had something called cerebral palsy," Sara said. "I cried, but if I had truly known what that meant I probably couldn't have made it." At the time Donnie and Sara didn't know much about cerebral palsy, but they knew two things irrevocably: "She was tough, and we loved her…and that was enough."

Simply put, cerebral palsy is a movement disorder that affects muscle tone, posture, and balance. It includes a wide array of symptoms and affects people differently with varying degrees of severity. Although the exact cause of cerebral palsy is debated, in general it is the result of damage to the brain's motor cortex—the part of the brain responsible for muscle control. Specialists believe this damage occurs at or shortly after birth. When doctors told Sara and Donnie that their baby had a brain bleed, they were describing an intracranial hemorrhage, which is not uncommon for premature babies. While some brain bleeds heal on their own, others can lead to hydrocephalus, literally "water on the brain." Hydrocephalus puts tremendous pressure on a baby's brain, which often leads to cerebral palsy.

By the time Amelia was five years old, she still wasn't walking. She practiced some with arm crutches, but mostly relied on crawling. It was around this time that Donnie and Sara heard about a groundbreaking surgery called a selective dorsal rhizotomy for children with CP. The threesome traveled to Charlotte for a consultation. After performing several tests on Amelia, the results were conclusive: she was a perfect candidate. The specialist warned Donnie and Sara that they were talking about major spinal cord surgery. The surgery had only been performed on seven people in the entire city of Charlotte. Amelia would need both physical and occupational therapy at least three times a week following surgery, and two sessions would have to be in Charlotte. "It was a big commitment to say the least," Sara remembers. But as they drove home, praying fervently for wisdom, one thing the specialist said rang louder than anything else: With this surgery, Amelia could learn to walk.

On October 30, 1990 Amelia became the eighth person in Charlotte to undergo a rhizotomy. The procedure involves testing individual nerve fibers in the lower spinal cord, which transmit sensation from the muscle to the spine. Based on an electrical response, the surgeon determines which abnormal fibers are causing spasticity and cuts them. Amelia's surgery took about six hours. When she came out of surgery, little Amelia—who only weighed twenty-five pounds at the time—had a six-inch scar down her lower back. She spent one night in intensive care and began therapy two days later. "They pushed her very hard," Sara recalls, "And the harder they pushed, the harder she pushed."

While most kindergarteners were coloring pictures and learning to play nicely at recess, Amelia was recovering from surgery, undergoing therapy, and learning to walk with arm crutches. Her mom credits their long drives to and from Charlotte for solidifying the deep bond they shared: "We bonded closely in the car. Even as a child, we had some deep talks. In some ways Amelia was always old." In the end the surgery and therapy paid off. Using arm crutches, Amelia became a proficient walker.

When it came to school, some things were easy for her and others were really hard. At her preschool evaluation, Donnie and Sara were told that Amelia would be below average, to which Sara promptly replied, "That just means she'll have to work harder and she'll be able to finish high school and go to college." The woman doing the evaluation bluntly responded, "Below average students don't go to college."

"She just didn't know my God," Sara remarks, looking back. Amelia graduated from high school in the top 20th percentile of her class. She was in National Honors Society and Beta Club, and went on to both college *and* seminary. Not to say it was an easy journey. Along the way, Amelia faced numerous setbacks both medically and emotionally as she learned to navigate a world that's often ignorant regarding those with disabilities.

For instance, in middle school she set her sights on becoming a cheerleader. The coaches were wonderful that year and welcomed her onto the team. So naturally, at high school orientation, Amelia marched straight to the cheerleading table. "I'm here for information about tryouts," she said brightly. The coach took one look at her arm crutches and said, "You do realize the requirements for being on our team, don't you?" She sent Amelia away without so much as a flyer. Amelia was crushed.

This time Sara marched straight to the principal's office. "Listen," she said. "I know my daughter has limitations. I'm not asking for special treatment. I'm not asking that you put her on that team. But she has a right to tryout just like everybody else."

"I can't do it!" Amelia cried later to her mom. "I can't go to tryouts and face that coach again!" After a long talk, Sara left the decision up to her daughter. On the morning of tryouts, Amelia showed up with her head held high—not because she thought she might make the team; she knew she wouldn't. She showed up because she had the right to try.

When we think of bravery, we usually picture victory: the hero riding into battle to save the day. But the only thing that takes more courage than walking into a situation hoping you will succeed, is walking into a situation knowing you will fail. Amelia was brave enough to fail. To dream big and risk big, because despite what stood against her, she knew God was for her. And His love made her brave.

Looking back, there's a tinge of laughter in Sara's voice as she recounts all of Amelia's ambitions. She joined service clubs, dove into church events, and was voted onto homecoming court her senior year. One of the most high energy ministries Amelia joined during high school was Young Life. One year as they prepared for a Young Life service project, an adult leader approached Sara. "Is your daughter the one with the crutches?" she asked.

"Yes," Sara replied, warily.

"And just what does she suppose she can do for the service project?" The leader demanded.

"Well," Sara said. "She can pick up sticks. She can fold laundry. And she can tell other people about Jesus…and isn't that the point of this whole thing anyway?"

Whenever I think about that conversation it makes me laugh! "I guess you're right," the leader replied meekly. Every time Amelia refused to squeeze into the narrow box people tried to cram her in, she broadened their perspective of God, herself, and others with disabilities.

The truth is, everybody dances differently. Some are slow and steady; others loud and vivacious. What matters is not *how* you dance through life, but *that* you dance. That you live an intentional life—unhindered by the past, engaged in the present, ambitious for the future. That's how Amelia danced in her life, not wasting one beat of her song. As you read her words you'll see her dance—sometimes small and ordinary like a child dancing in the rain, and sometimes fierce and indomitable like a fighter dancing in the ring. I wonder, what would it look like to dance a little more in my life? In yours?

MY STORY

All my life I have tried to live by Philippians 4:4, "Rejoice in the Lord always, again I say rejoice." But it hasn't always been easy. I was born three months premature, and because of that developed a disability called cerebral palsy. Living with CP over the years has definitely been a challenge, but Christ has been with me every step of the way. I accepted Jesus Christ as my Lord and Savior when I was eight years old, and that was the best decision I ever made. Thankfully, I am blessed to have parents who love Jesus Christ more than anything else, and have always exemplified Him. In the years to come, it was that strong faith that carried us through.

Up until I was in the fifth grade, my life consisted of school, physical and occupational therapy, and a multitude of surgeries. I did not live the same type of life that the majority of kids my age lived, and went through a major depression in my elementary and middle school years because I did not understand why I was different. My CP affects the way that I walk, and I am required to use arm-crutches for assistance. Because the other kids my age did not understand this, they would choose not to talk to me and make fun of me. I would come home every day in tears. But when I started to mentally comprehend Christ and His character, seeing myself as a true daughter of the King, my perspective changed. A passage of Scripture that has always encouraged me is Psalm 139: 13-16:

> For you created my inmost being, you knit me together in my mother's womb. I praise you because I am fearfully and wonderfully made. Your works are wonderful and I know that full well. My frame was not hidden from you when I was made in that secret place, when I was woven together in the depths of the earth your eyes saw my unformed body; all the days ordained for me were written in your book before one of them came to be.

I began to realize who I was IN Christ, and I no longer worried about what others thought. My main desire became to know Christ better each day and to live a completely surrendered life for Him. I knew that God had a purpose for my life and that His purpose was greater than any struggle I would face.

2 Corinthians 12:9 states, "My grace is sufficient for thee: for my strength is made perfect in weakness. Most gladly therefore will I rather glory in my infirmities, that the power of Christ may rest upon me." My life is living proof of God's grace. Doctors told my parents that I would never graduate from high school, but because of Him I

did, and went on to graduate from college too. It has been God's grace that has sustained me through all of the adversity I faced as an adult in society and the work force. It is also because of God's grace that despite my daily health challenges, God gives me the strength to serve Him in a ministry that I love and to rejoice in Him day after day.

God daily reminds me that I am not alone in my suffering, and that it was because of His suffering on the cross that I am able to live this beautiful life. God has called me to a life set apart for Him, which means living a joyful life always, no matter what comes my way.

In Scripture God has always used the example of Paul to encourage me. Paul experienced many hardships and sufferings while following Christ, and Scripture tells us that he dealt with a "thorn in the flesh." But through it all he remained joyful. Paul tells us the secret to this joy and contentment in a letter he wrote to the church of Philippi:

> I am not saying this because I am in need, for I have learned to be content in whatever the circumstances. I know what it is to be in need, and I know what it is to have plenty. I have learned the secret of being content in any and every situation, whether fed or hungry, whether in plenty or in want. I can do all things through him who gives me strength (Philippians 4:11-13).

Throughout my life I have learned that no matter what is going on in and around you, you can still have joy even in the worst of times. That is when Christ can shine the most. It is easy to be selfish and get caught up in what we want. It is also easy to think that a joyful life is defined by a series of happy moments and fulfilled desires. However, life is really defined by the work Jesus Christ is doing in you, and how He allows the "not so good moments" to mature you. In some of my hardest seasons, I have experienced some of my sweetest moments with Jesus.

Every one of us—no matter who we are—has struggles. However, we are called to glorify God with the life that He has given us. I want to encourage you to not let your circumstances define you and steal your joy. Be thankful for what God has given you. Know that He loves you and created you for His purpose. Spend time reading His Word daily and ask Him to give you His never-ending joy. If you do this, the weight of your worries will lessen, and life will suddenly seem brighter. Be encouraged that in His presence there is fullness of joy (Psalm 16:11), and that God works out *all* things for the good of those who love Him (Romans 8:28).

BE OBEDIENT

Obedience. Obedience can be scary and peaceful all at the same time. Over the last year—and especially in the last several months—God has taught me so much. January 23, 2015 changed my life forever. That was the day I had my colon removed. It was also the start of a six-week hospital stay, and the scariest time of my life. It was truly miraculous that I survived, and during this time I became more real and raw with God than I have ever been before.

For years God has been calling me to share the story of His amazing grace in my life as a writer and speaker. The problem is I hate public speaking, even though when I was in college my public speaking professor told me I had a gift and a story to be shared. Nevertheless, when I was done with that class I washed my hands of public speaking for good.

God has such a sense of humor. For the last several years I have worked for speakers and writers instead of being one. I just knew (and wanted really badly to think) that my ministry was only behind the scenes. Although I have loved every minute of my work with Hollywood comedians, there has always been a thought in the back of my mind: "God is wanting me to do more." In the quiet time of my recovery, I've heard that still small voice again.

If I have learned one truth through this surgery and recovery, it is that life is too short to be disobedient to God's calling. Fast forward to the present. I am still very much in recovery mode, and physically not able to go back to work or start a speaking ministry yet. However, I want Jesus to know that I am willing.

~

Life is too short to be disobedient to God's calling.

~

What Jesus wants most from us is a willing heart, ready to be molded by Him for His glory. I want to offer my body as a living sacrifice to do whatever God sees fit for my life from this moment forward because any fear on my part is smaller than the power of God. Just as he did for Moses, Abraham, and countless others in the Bible, He can equip and enable me to do whatever He asks me to do. He will equip you as well; you just have to be willing to let Him lead your life. What is He asking you to do today? Is there an area in your life where you are resisting obedience to Him? Don't waste your life running from obedience. Heed His wisdom and commands.

DEALING WITH STEREOTYPES

Stereotypes have and always will be in existence. Unfortunately, that doesn't make them any less annoying or hurtful. No one is perfect and I think if we were honest, we would admit that we've all been guilty of stereotyping, whether intentionally or unintentionally.

As someone who has been a victim of stereotyping, I try to look at people for who they really are rather than judging them for who I think they are. Because of my CP, I walk with arm-crutches. Over the years I have received special and somewhat degrading treatment because of this. There is rarely a day that goes by when I don't receive "the look" from someone when I'm out in public. After dealing with this for thirty years I've grown to ignore it, but nevertheless it's there. When I refer to "the look" I am talking about the gaze or stare that I receive from another person, which usually displays pity. I realize that the people giving these looks do not mean any harm; they're just not sure how to respond to me.

A recent example of this happened last weekend. I went out with my mom to the movies and to do some shopping. While shopping I used a wheelchair, because since the surgery my energy is not what it used to be. All through the day I just kept noticing "the looks." It was stare after stare, and after a while one just wonders —"Okay seriously, have you people never seen a wheelchair before? Do I have something on my face or in my hair?"

I used to travel frequently for my job, and a lot of times at the airport the easiest way for me to get assistance was to use a wheelchair. On my last flight, during the security process, the officers did not listen to anything I had to say. Instead, they spoke to my friend and told her to tell me certain things. That was when my friend and I both spoke up insisting that I could speak for myself and that I had a mind of my own. Just because someone uses crutches or a wheelchair for assistance, does not mean they are less independent or successful than other people. It also does not indicate that a person has a mental disability along with the physical one, even though that is a common misconception. Some people can look past it and others cannot. I had someone tell me once that he thought disabled people wanted pity, to which I responded, "No we just want normal treatment."

I am fortunate that I have friends and family who love, support, and encourage me. I learned a long time ago not to let these stereotypes define who I am. Jesus Christ defines me and I am so thankful for His love and grace. I know I am not the only person struggling with stereotypes today and I want to encourage you not to let stereotypes and poor treatment from others define you. You are worth way more than that!

Everyone has a disability, some are just more visible than others. I want to challenge everyone this week to look past appearances and stereotypes and treat others the way you would want to be treated.

FEAR

Fear. All throughout Scripture Christ commands us not to fear. However, as humans that is easier said than done. Sometimes the circumstances of life can be so overwhelming, and you don't know how to be unafraid. Sometimes the future can seem so dark and scary that you don't want to even move, for fear of what will or won't happen next. It would be so much easier if we could just know what was around the bend. But as one of my favorite Amy Grant songs says,

> *Sometimes, it's better not to know,*
> *which way it's going to go,*
> *what will die and what will grow,*
> *it's better not to know.*[1]

Those are simple but very true words. We may not know what is next in life, but there is One who does, and His name is Jesus.

---

[1] Amy Grant. *How Mercy Looks From Here*. Sparrow Records, 2013.

I have never been more grateful for His presence than I have been in this season. If you have been following my journey for the past year or so, you know that I have been having some serious health problems. In January of 2015, I had my colon removed and following that spent over five weeks in the hospital due to life-threatening complications.

I underwent a massive recovery process, but in November things started to get worse again. After several months of pain, and problems with my ostomy[2], I saw my surgeon in March and he told me news that I didn't want to hear—more surgery. More surgery for me could be complicated and very risky, but it has to be done. He said there are possibly partial blockages and scar tissue, but he will not know the extent of what is going on until he goes in. Due to my previous surgeries, this one is not going to be easy, and there are more risks involved than normal. We are not sure what to expect or even how long I will be in the hospital. Because of what happened last year, not knowing more details has been hard, and I have been fearful of the outcome.

However, this week the Lord has so gently and lovingly reminded me of all the times in His Word where He commands us not to be afraid. Jesus is my everything, and He deserves my full obedience in all circumstances. No matter what occurs, God wants me to obey His Word and trust Him. The situation is out of my control so worrying about it is not going to change anything. But there is one thing I can control and that is my choice to trust the

---

[2] An ostomy is a procedure that allows bodily waste to pass through a surgically created opening on the abdomen (known as a stoma) and into a pouch on the outside of the body.

Lord and surrender my will to His, which means trusting Him with my life and believing that He is powerful enough to handle what comes my way.

Lately, as I have been meditating on different Scripture passages related to this, God has given me a peace that passes all understanding. My circumstances have not changed, but my heart has. As 1 John 4:18 says, "Perfect love casts out all fear." Other verses that have encouraged me are:

So do not fear, for I am with you; do not be dismayed, for I am your God. I will strengthen you and help you; I will uphold you with my righteous right hand (Isaiah 41:10).

Peace is what I leave with you; it is my own peace that I give you. I do not give it as the world does. Do not be worried and upset; do not be afraid (John 14:27).

Have I not commanded you? Be strong and courageous. Do not be terrified; do not be discouraged, for the Lord your God will be with you wherever you go (Joshua 1:9).

Therefore do not worry about tomorrow, for tomorrow will worry about itself. Each day has enough trouble of its own (Matthew 6:34).

LIVING IN THE NOW

"Courage, dear heart."[3] That is one of my favorite quotes from C.S. Lewis, and I have been reminded of it a lot lately. When I think about people who have courage, I think about people like Corrie Ten Boom who was imprisoned in a concentration camp, or Elisabeth Elliot who ministered to the same people who murdered her husband. I think of Esther Ahn Kim who stood up for her faith when the Japanese took control of Korea, or Amy Carmichael who moved to India alone and rescued orphans.

All of these women displayed courage in major ways, and when I was younger I wanted to be just like them. I still want to be like them. They are some of my greatest heroes. Many times I've thought, "If only I could go overseas and be a missionary then I would really be courageous...then I would feel purposeful." Or I've thought, "If only I was married and serving my husband and fulfilling the ministry God has for a family, then I would be living out a worthwhile calling." I've thought, "If only I were able to travel

---

[3] CS Lewis, *The Voyage of the Dawn Treader*. (New York: HarperCollins, 1952).

more and not be bogged down with health problems, then I would meet more people and have more career opportunities, and I would be secure."

None of these things are bad and certainly they are God's calling for some people. But right now in my life, they are not my calling. I can live in the land of "if only" all day long, but that's not going to change the reality of the "now." I was praying the other day and said, "God, if only I was in better physical health, just think of all I could do for you and all the places we could go. Lord, if you would let that occur that would be wonderful." Yes, it would be wonderful, but the Lord whispered back:

> Yes, my child, but what about the now? What if the calling I am asking of you is this hard season, right here, right now. It takes just as much courage to stay put in the difficulty as it does to be on-the-go doing something else. That 'something else' has its own difficulty as well.

The Lord reminded me that He does not want me to live in the land of "if onlys;" He wants me to live in the "now." He has as much purpose in the "nows" as He does in the "if onlys," even though our human hearts do not always believe that to be true. In those quiet moments the Lord said, "Take Courage, dear heart. Take courage; your life is worth a great price to Me and you have an enormous purpose today. Believe that, daughter."

Friend, if you are struggling like me right now—and if your life has not turned out the way you thought it would—God still has a

~

It takes just as much courage to stay put in the difficulty as it does to be on-the-go doing something else.

~

plan and a purpose for you. You just have to be willing to accept what He has given you and rejoice in the now. As I am learning, He will use you in ways you least expect.

DISABILITY LIMITS MARRIAGE CHOICES

Recently I found an article online from India titled "Disability Limits Marriage Choices."[4] It caught my attention so I continued reading. According to the article, people with a physical disability have a harder time finding a mate and getting married. The reason for this is because a lot of people in society cannot look past the appearance of a disability. Polls were taken from the US, UK, Canada, Middle East, SE Asia, Australia, and New Zealand. The results were as follows: 59% of women and 48% of men refuse to marry anyone with a physical disability, and 34% of women and 37% of men said it depended on the type and extent of disability. Only 7% of women and 15% of men said that they would marry a person with a physical disability.

I wish that I could say that I find these results surprising, but I do not. As a person who has lived with a physical disability for 26 years, I am well aware of how people think. Do I think it is

---

[4] Meenakshi Sinha. "Diability Limits Marriage Choices: Online Survey," *Times of India,* May 2011. https://timesofindia.indiatimes.com/india/Disability-limits-marriage-choices-Online-survey/articleshow/8245445.cms

impossible to find a mate if one has a disability? Absolutely not! I sincerely hope that I get married someday. However, I do think that a person with a disability may have to wait longer to find the right person and get married. Still, it's possible. I have met several couples with great marriages in which one of the spouses has a disability. Although a person who becomes involved with someone with a disability might face certain criticisms, such as "Why would you want to date a disabled person?" or "Wouldn't you rather marry someone without a disability?" and "Do you know what you are getting into?" These questions all stem from stereotypes people have of those with disabilities.

Recently, I saw an excellent example of this in a movie called "Listen to Your Heart." The main character in the movie dates a girl who is deaf. At the beginning of their relationship, his friends question what he is doing, urging him to find someone else. He responds by saying, "I am not going to miss out on something great just because it might be hard." What a great viewpoint to have in all relationships! So many people miss out on great friendships because they cannot get past a stereotype. Have you stereotyped someone in your life? How might you begin looking past outward appearances into the hearts of others?

CLOTHED IN CHRIST

"Therefore, as God's chosen people, holy and dearly loved, clothe yourselves with compassion, kindness, humility, gentleness and patience. Bear with each other and forgive one another if any of you has a grievance against someone. Forgive as the Lord forgave you. And over all these virtues put on love, which binds them all together in perfect unity. Let the peace of Christ rule in your hearts, since as members of one body you were called to peace. And be thankful" (Colossians 3:12-15).

As a woman I love a good outfit. I enjoy shopping, putting together outfits for special occasions, and feeling pretty. What woman doesn't, right? While there is nothing wrong with desiring to look nice outwardly, so many times we fail to work on our inward appearance. If we're honest, we could all use a character check occasionally, and that is exactly what the passage in Colossians 3 gives us.

Verse 12 begins by stating, "Therefore, as God's chosen people, holy and dearly loved..." This statement presents the entire motivation for why God's children should be clothed with the qualities that are mentioned in the following verses. We are chosen and beloved by God, and as mentioned in Deuteronomy, God calls us His treasured possession.

No matter who we are or what we have done, God loves us with an everlasting love. The day we accept Him as Savior, our lives become new. As believers we are to put aside the former ways of life and display the love of Christ by having compassion, kindness, humility, gentleness, patience, forgiveness, love, and peace. These qualities are not always easy to live out, especially during hard seasons. When we are not actively pursuing Jesus and His Word, we cannot glorify him in the way that He deserves. To another person, the life we live may seem perfect. However, even though we may appear to have it all together on the outside, if others do not see Jesus in us, then nothing else matters. This passage calls each of us to live out these characteristics regardless of our circumstances.

Also, it is important for each of us to be on guard focusing daily on renewing our mind, and guarding our gate. The things we allow in, will eventually spill over into how we live. If we are lazy guards, we will become consumed with anger, bitterness, and selfishness instead of love, gentleness, and compassion.

GOD IS FAITHFUL

One week ago today, my dear friend Erin got married. It was such a joyous day and I was so thankful to be part of it as a bridesmaid. That day was an answer to many prayers and evidence of God's faithfulness to both Erin and Jeremy. Even in crazy hurricane weather, with power that did not come on until thirty minutes before the ceremony, in the end all was well and beautiful. It was such a great time to see and catch up with old friends.

Weddings are also a reminder to me of God's faithfulness and the great love He has for His children. We are His bride—His beloved—and He pursues us daily. He is always standing at the end of the aisle with a smile, ready for us to come to Him and commit. He treasures us and fulfills our greatest desires with Himself. He is truly the greatest lover of all time and all other love is second to His.

God is my rock and even in the midst of this season of difficulty, He has shown up and reminded me that He is faithful in ALL things. He is the faithful Leader in my life and has great plans for me even when I do not understand. He rejoices in me and wants me to rejoice in Him. Isaiah 62:5 states, "As a bridegroom rejoices over his bride, so will your God rejoice over you." This is the message God is reminding me of as I spend time in His Word today. On the days when I feel tired, overwhelmed, or lonely, He reminds me that He is all I need, and He loves me with an unfailing love! When I think of God in this light it is hard to be discouraged because His faithfulness is so evident. Take a moment and dwell on God's faithfulness in your life today and thank Him for all the ways He has been there for you.

MORNINGS WITH NEHEMIAH

Lately I've been studying the book of Nehemiah and wanted to reflect on what I'm learning. As I read through Chapter 1, I immediately notice Nehemiah's willingness to cry out to God. In the first chapter Nehemiah finds out the devastating news that the wall of Jerusalem has been destroyed. Where does he turn first? He begins to pray and repent of his people's sins, crying out to the Lord to have mercy on His people. He has a repentant heart, and in his distress, focuses on Christ. Nehemiah repents for his people and then asks the Lord to show him mercy in the sight of the king (1:6-11). God grants Nehemiah's request. The King listens to Nehemiah and supports his mission to go rebuild the wall for his people.

Have you ever viewed God as a last resort? And yet as believers, God should always be the One we turn to first—in hardship and in joy. Not friends. Not family. God.

Why? Because God is our Heavenly Father, and He is a jealous God. He delights in communion with us and desires for us to come to Him with everything. He is always ready to listen, forgive, and guide.

One of the phrases that repeatedly stuck out to me in Nehemiah, is "Guard your gates!" Throughout the book, as Nehemiah and his men rebuild the gates of the city, they recognize that these gates protect the people. Just as they built gates around their city, we must build gates around our minds.`32w1

One of the best ways to guard ourselves daily is by taking everything to God in prayer. Recently, this has been such a good reminder for me. I have been overwhelmed and anxious regarding my health, but when I read Nehemiah I'm reminded to pray and offer my health back to God. My situation hasn't changed. But by praying and guarding my mind in this way I am able to keep going, carried by the strength of Jesus.

At some point today find time to talk with the Lord, even if it is just for a few minutes. Time with Him can change your perspective of an entire day. Instead of calling your friend and sharing your latest work drama, call out to God instead. The same God whom Nehemiah trusted, can also help you. You just have to let Him in.

LOVING THE UNLOVABLE

If we're honest, we can all think of people from different seasons of life that have been hard to love. Maybe it's that person from high school who sought to make your life miserable every day, the neighbor who is always stirring up drama, the co-worker that loves to point out your flaws, or that one family member who is always telling you that you're not good enough. Of course there are also extreme examples of those who are hard to love, like people who commit murder or those who participate in terrible acts of violence.

However, the unlovable includes not only enemies but outcasts. Maybe the thought of befriending an unlikely person makes you uncomfortable. As Christians, the Bible speaks specifically to this topic. God is very clear throughout the Word that we are to love everyone.

No matter who you consider unlovable, or what they have done—God calls us to love them anyway. I know from personal experience that can be a hard pill to swallow. Certainly God cannot expect me to love someone who made fun of me everyday for years and made me out to be a laughingstock, right? Wrong. In Mark 12:31 Jesus commands, "Love your neighbor as yourself." Also, Matthew 5:44 states, "But I say to you, love your enemies and pray for those who persecute you." Jesus was the perfect example of this. He was persecuted and scorned, but He still loved. In John 13 when Jesus washed the disciples feet, He knew that some in the room would later betray Him. However, He still lovingly served them.

Christ could consider each and every one of us unlovable because it was our sin that He died for, but instead He loves us with an everlasting love that we do not deserve. Being a friend to the unlovable takes on a whole new meaning when I think of the sacrificial love of Jesus. He is the example we should follow with everyone we come in contact with. Our purpose should be to love like Jesus loves. Instead of treating others as an enemy or an outcast, we should look at them from God's perspective.

Everyone deserves to hear the Gospel and have a chance to know Jesus as their Savior. This includes our enemies, and we need to live our lives in a compelling way for the sake of the gospel. Who is one unlovable person in your life right now? How might you take a step to demonstrate compassion or forgiveness toward them?

RESTLESS

Lately, I have been restless. I could sit here and tell you that my restlessness stems from major health problems this year, or the fact that I'm single, or because I've had to put my job on hold. Do those things contribute to my restlessness? Yes, but they are not the primary cause of it. The main reason for my discontentment is that I am not trusting God as I should. I'm a planner who likes to have everything figured out. Yet here I am in a season where nothing seems to be figured out. But I think that's exactly where God wants me.

It's so easy to feel content when all of my plans are working out, but that's just it—the focus is on me and not God. I have been craving peace lately, but in my finite ways, my mindset is that peace will come when things in life work out. That is wrong thinking. The Bible says that God offers us perfect peace regardless of our circumstances (Isaiah 26:3).

It is such a comfort to know that even when I am restless, God is not. In order to have peace, all I have to do is trust. When you choose to love Christ above all else, peace will rule in your heart no matter your circumstances. My prayer today is that I have the Christlike attitude that Paul had when he stated in Philippians 4:12, "I know what it is to be in need, and I know what it is to have plenty. I have learned the secret of being content in any and every situation, whether fed or hungry, whether living in plenty or in want." Paul's contentment was found in Christ alone. That was all he needed, and is all you or I need. If you are restless today, give your restlessness to Christ and He will give you His perfect peace. Nothing or no one could be better than that.

LITTLE MERCIES

In my last post I talked about feeling restless and God's peace. Through His peace, God has been reminding me daily of things to be thankful for that I like to call "little mercies." No matter how mundane or hard our lives may seem at the moment, because of Christ we always have something to be thankful for. This summer I have decided to start journaling more and be intentional about recording these little mercies each day. This exercise helps me keep perspective when things seem otherwise gloomy. I would like to share some of my "little mercies" from today, and challenge you to take a moment to consider and be thankful for the little mercies God is bringing your way.

- My sweet Savior Jesus Christ
- Awesome parents who I consider my best friends
- Dear friends who I can share life with and who love, listen, and pray for me when times get hard

– Nurses who daily help make my daily life easier during this season

– Jon Guerra's new album, "Little Songs." I think this is my theme music for the summer now. Why did I wait so long to listen to his music?? So good! Favorite songs are "Nothing Better" and "Wherever You Are"

– Psalms – I have been reading through them lately and they are a balm to my soul. Psalm 91:4 has greatly encouraged me the last couple of days. It states, "He will cover you with his feathers. He will shelter you with his wings. His faithful promises are your armor and protection."

– "I Come Quietly To Meet You" Devotional by Amy Carmichael – Later in her life, Amy had some serious health problems that left her homebound for years.

– Diet Sundrop – What can I say? I am addicted to this soda. I am definitely a Carolina girl and this is my summer treat.

– My pool, which is my favorite dwelling place for the summer especially over the last week or so during what feels to be the hottest time of the year. Also, it has been a great form of exercise for me as I have been recovering.

Okay, now it is your turn. What little mercies has God given you this week? Reflect on them this weekend.

HAPPY VALENTINE'S DAY

Today is Valentine's Day. For many it's a day to celebrate with the ones you love. However, not everyone has a spouse or significant other, and a day filled with lots of love, flowers, and chocolate, can be very depressing for single folks. While others are waiting to receive a special gift, or go on a special date, singles go into the day not expecting anything. For us, it is another reminder of what we long for but do not have.

As I have been pondering this over the past few days, the Lord has gently reminded me that on Valentine's Day I am not alone because I have Him. He is greater than a boyfriend, husband, friend, or any gift that I could ever receive. He is the greatest gift. He is enough. I have everything I need in Him. As Isaiah 54:5 states, "For your Maker is your husband—the LORD Almighty is his name—the Holy One of Israel is your Redeemer; he is called the God of all the earth."

Because of Jesus, I am able to go through life completely fulfilled and content even if He never chooses to bless me with an earthly love story. No love story is complete without Him because He is the greatest lover of all time. With or without a husband, Jesus should always be the greatest lover of our souls. Nothing or no one should ever take the place of His rule in our hearts and lives.

During the past week, the Lord has brought to mind several verses that display His great love for us. I am calling these my "Love Letters from Jesus." Take a moment to read them and be encouraged.

~

When we put our relationship with Jesus above all else, He makes all of our other relationships even more beautiful.

~

Whether you are married or single today, evaluate your relationship with the Lord. Are you allowing Him to be the Lord of your life? Do you prioritize His relationship as the most important one in your life?

When we put our relationship with Jesus above all else, He makes all of our other relationships even more beautiful. If you're single today, please know that you are not alone. Jesus loves you with a perfect and everlasting love. Unlike people, He will never let you down. Allow these words from Scripture to penetrate your heart and mind, and choose to believe them:

"I have loved you with an everlasting love." Jeremiah 31:3

"But now, this is what the LORD says—He who created you, Jacob, He who formed you, Israel: Do not fear, for I have redeemed you; I have summoned you by name; you are mine." Isaiah 43:1

"He has brought me to his banquet hall, and His ban
love." Song of Solomon 2:4

"The Lord your God is with you, the Mighty Warrior who saves. He will take great delight in you; in His love He will no longer rebuke you, but will rejoice over you with singing." Zephaniah 3:17

"For you are a people holy to the LORD your God. The LORD your God has chosen you out of all the peoples on the face of the earth to be His people, His treasured possession." Deuteronomy 7:6

"I am my beloved's and my beloved is mine." Song of Solomon 6:3

"For your Maker is your husband–the LORD Almighty is His name– the Holy One of Israel is your Redeemer; He is called the God of all the earth." Isaiah 54:5

FEARFULLY AND WONDERFULLY MADE

"I praise you because I am fearfully and wonderfully made; your works are wonderful, I know that full well" (Psalm 139:14). Some days it's hard to "know full well" that we are fearfully and wonderfully made. At least it is for me. Since my surgery, I have had issues with my weight and retaining fluid. One day my weight is up and another it's down. Similarly, my hair has yet to recover from all the trauma I have been through. "Bad hair day" does not even begin to describe the state my hair is in. Even my lovely mother who is a hair-dresser has no clue what to do with it. (I know I'm a hot mess on the days when even my mom can't work miracles!)

Then there's the issue of "the bag." I have an ileostomy bag due to my colon being removed, and do not worry, I will spare you most of the details. However, this bag causes disasters from time to time, and it has caused a major upset to my clothes closet. A lot of my clothes do not work anymore because of this, or rather, they don't look the same. The first day I got ready to go somewhere post-op and post hospital, I had a meltdown in my closet and yelled, "I have absolutely no clothes to wear!!" Many would think I was exaggerating, but it was true. Well, mostly true!

Although, once I calmed down, I realized that this just gives me an excuse to shop and what girl doesn't like the thought of that? It also helps when your best friend's family owns the cutest clothing boutique, and she immediately drops what she is doing to help me find some new clothes. That is a true friend right there. Love you, Sara!

Seriously though, I know all women have days where we don't feel beautiful enough. We go through seasons where we feel like nothing is right...which takes me back to Psalm 139:14. It is true, even when we don't "feel" like it, we are "fearfully and wonderfully made."

There is nothing about our bodies that God has not created. There's nothing He doesn't understand about us. We are made in His glorious image, and because of that we are beautiful.

It is because of that truth that I am able to get up every day and move forward with confidence even in the midst of major changes to my life physically, emotionally, and spiritually. In the midst of all my junk, God is here and He is giving me the strength to carry on. Dear sisters, He will give you the strength to do the same.

PRAYER, FUTURE HUSBANDS, AND SINGLENESS

I am 30 years old and have been praying for my future husband since I was 12. That is 18 years of praying for a man I have never met (or at least I don't think we've met). Lately, I have wondered if I am called to a life of singleness. Leslie Ludy frequently tells the story of her sister-in-law Krissy, who was single for many years before meeting her husband. Before marriage people would often ask Krissy, "Are you called to a life of singleness?" Her response was always, "Today I am." I love that perspective, and it is now my response as well. Since I am single today then I am called by God to be single in this season unless He decides to send me a husband.

One fact that I have learned over the years is that Jesus Christ is always enough and is my ultimate fulfillment. Sure, there are days when being single is really hard, and the struggle is very real, but that is when Jesus meets me in my need and gives me grace upon grace. Because of His grace, I have the strength to (most importantly) live for Jesus, and to honor my future husband if God wills for me to be married one day.

Proverbs 31:12 states that a wife of noble character is to bring her husband "good not harm *all* the days of her life." This verse does not only apply to women who have already met their spouses, but to single women as well. We should be living all of our life in a way that ultimately glorifies the Lord, and also in a way that would be faithful to a future husband. One way to live this out is by praying for your future husband even before you meet him. Even if one never marries, your prayers will not be wasted.

Several years ago I was reminded of the power of prayer in this area after hearing a friend's testimony. She shared that one night she woke up at 3am and felt the Lord telling her to pray for her future husband. She spent the remainder of the night in prayer because she knew he was in trouble. She continued to pray for him daily after that. A year later, when she was getting to know the man who is now her husband, he told her that he was involved in a car accident that almost took his life. As he told her the details of how it happened, it was exactly the date and time that the Lord woke her up to pray. When I heard this story I was reminded that God values and honors our prayers for a husband even when we cannot see what He is doing.

One of my favorite books on this topic is titled *Praying For Your Future Husband* by Robin Jones Gunn and Tricia Goyer. The authors share Biblical encouragement and wisdom on how to pray for your husband and prepare your heart for his. It also gives suggestions for how to pray for your sisters in Christ. Spend some time this week in prayer for your future husband as well as your fellow sisters as we are trying to be the women God has called us to be. Here are some ideas for prayer points:

- **Pray for his Salvation** – Pray that your future husband will surrender his life to Jesus Christ. While you're at it, pray for those within your circles of influence—friends, neighbors, and family members. Salvation is the greatest gift of all.

- **Pray for Wisdom and Guidance** – Pray that your future husband will have supernatural wisdom to discern God's will for his life. Pray that God would direct his steps (Proverbs 19:21) and begin molding him into the leader God has called him to be, even now.

- **Pray for Purity** – Pray for the strength and conviction to flee temptation. Pray that he would grow in faithfulness to God in big and little ways everyday. Pray that he would practice confession and repentance when he sins (Psalm 32:5). Pray the same thing for yourself and those you love.

- **Pray for Protection** – Pray for physical, emotional, mental, and spiritual protection for your future husband. Pray that he would know and cling to the truth, which has the power to set us free (John 8:32). Pray that he would be a man devoted to the Word (John 17:17) and prayer (Colossians 4:2). Pray the same thing for yourself and those you love.

- **Pray for Encouragement** – Pray that your future husband would grow in trusting God daily, for "the Lord's unfailing love surrounds the man who trusts in Him" (Psalm 32:10). As he faces challenges, pray that God would encourage his heart (2 Corinthians 4:8-9), strengthen his faith, and uphold him with His hand (Psalm 37:24). Pray the same for yourself, your family, and friends.

GRACE UPON GRACE

As most of you know by now, I am recovering from a couple major surgeries from back in January and February. It has been a long journey since then. Because of complications with my ostomy, I have have had recurring bladder infections, and these infections have been making me very sick. Like, in-bed-all-day-don't-want-to-move kind of sick. This has been happening over the last couple of months and on Friday I woke up with the same heaviness that I always feel when a new infection is starting. So for the past few days I have not felt the best, but it is in these times that I feel the Lord's strength and grace the most. When I have no strength left He is right there, ready for me to take from Him. I have had the song "When it Hurts" by Hillsong United on repeat this week. Some of my favorite lines from it are:

> *Even when my strength is lost I'll praise you*
> *Even when I have no song I'll praise you*
> *Even when it's hard to find the words,*

louder then I'll sing your praise.[5]

This has been my prayer to the Lord for days. I have also been reminded of John 1:16 which states, "For from His fullness we have all received, grace upon grace." Grace upon Grace! I just love that. It is never-ending, and there is always a big enough supply for whatever circumstances we are facing.

I know I am not the only one struggling today, and I am praying for you, my sweet reader. If you haven't done so today, take a moment and reach out to Jesus. Pray for Him to give you His strength and to lavish you with grace upon grace. I promise you that He will not disappoint. He will meet you right where you are and give you His peace to get through your current situation.

---

[5] Hillsong United. *Empires.* Sparrow Records, 2015. CD.

THIS IS MY AFRICA

This past weekend has been a humbling one, and I needed this timely reminder of what Jesus has done for me. No matter how many trials I face, there is nothing He does not understand due to His death and resurrection. Instead of complaining about my current season, I realized that I am so undeserving of the Lord's grace and love. He deserves all my praises not just when life is good but in the sufferings as well. It doesn't matter how unfaithful we are, the Lord is always faithful to us. His love knows no end. Certain circumstances may make it difficult for us to view life from this perspective, but the Lord uses all things — joys as well as sorrows — for His glory.

As Philippians 1:21 states, "To live is Christ and to die is gain." It should be my privilege to serve and rejoice in Christ on a daily basis despite the struggles I face. I may never know the reasons God allows me to suffer in this life, but I will understand when I get to Heaven and that is all the explanation I need.

The Lord never stops working in our lives no matter how hard some days can be. Because of my chronic infections, I spend the majority of my days at home laying in my hospital bed. This allows me a lot of time to read, pray, and dwell on both the struggles and joys of life. On my sickest days I tend to worry and fret about what is to come and create many "what-if" scenarios in my mind. Last week in my pondering, I told God, "Lord if I were healthy, I would be serving you in Africa or somewhere overseas. If I could, and if I were healthy just think of all the ministries I would be involved with!"

Then the Lord hit me hard with His response. After thinking and praying, I felt the Lord say:

> Amelia, you said you would be willing to go anywhere and do anything for Me; so how about living fully right where you are? This is where I want you and am using you for My glory. This is your ministry. I am using you more here than I would be using you in Africa because you are not meant for Africa—You are meant for here. This is your Africa. So child, be obedient to Me and share what I am teaching you during this season.

Wow, what a wakeup call from King Jesus. While overseas ministries are much needed, and working in a church ministry full-time would be wonderful, God is showing me once again that I can be in ministry for Him even from a hospital bed. This is not what I had in mind by the time I was 32, but this is where God has me. Therefore, I desire to be obedient and to make the best of the life He has given. As Scripture points out, God often uses our weaknesses for His strength.

~

How about living fully right where you are?

~

You may not be dealing with health issues, but I know we all have our trials. I want you to be encouraged that God is using you even on the worst days. He loves you more than you can imagine so continue to press into Him and allow Him to work. Throw out your expectations and desires. Let go of the pride that's holding you back. Instead, surrender to what the Lord has for you. Only then will you be content.

LAUGH A LITTLE MORE

"I saw more clearly than ever that the first great and primary business to which I ought to attend every day was to have my soul happy in the Lord. The first thing to be concerned about was not how much I might serve the Lord, how I might glorify the Lord; but how I might get my soul into a happy state, and how my inner man might be nourished."

~George Mueller

WHY AMELIA LAUGHED

Around the time she was in third grade, the full weight of Amelia's disability settled squarely on her young shoulders. "It was the first time she really realized she was different, and it wasn't going away," Sara recalls. "One of the hardest conversations we ever had was when I told her that unless God performed a miracle, she would never be better." Amelia, who had been believing God for healing, began to slip into depression.

One day while driving in the car together, Sara had a life-changing conversation with her daughter. "She was so bitter," Sara remembers. "I told her that it was her choice. She could let the devil steal every bit of joy she ever had, or she could choose to find joy no matter what."

"Nobody can make that choice except you," Sara said soberly to the little girl in the backseat. Amelia talked about that moment for the rest of her life. It was the day she decided joy was worth fighting for. "Not to say she didn't have her hard days," Sara adds. "She did. But I can honestly say she always chose joy."

One of Amelia's greatest hurdles was her neurogenic bladder. Because the brain is the control center for the entire body, a disability affecting the motor cortex has implications for many bodily functions, including emptying and controlling the bladder. So in seventh grade Amelia underwent bladder augmentation. The surgery was extensive, akin to building a completely new bladder. From then on, she had to self-catheterize through her belly-button every four to six hours. It was major responsibility for a thirteen-year-old, but Amelia took it in stride.

Things that were minor setbacks for others completely upended Amelia's life. When she got mono during her junior year of high school, she had to be homebound for several months, and then go to school part-time until she fully recovered.

By the time college rolled around, Amelia knew she wanted to pursue a communications degree. She chose a small Bible college in Columbia, South Carolina, and set to work moving into the dorm, making friends, and studying for classes. As an assignment for one of her classes, she signed up for the Hollywood prayer network, where she met a woman whose daughter was pursuing an acting career. Over time Amelia and the budding actress's mother became prayer partners. The experience struck a chord in Amelia, and she began to do what she did best: dream.

"Mom," Amelia said one day. "I want to work in Hollywood."

Sara—ever the champion of her daughter's dreams—knew that once in a while she had to tether her child to reality. "Honey," she said. "You're a small town girl with a disability. How in the world are you going to work in that industry? Why would you even want to?"

"I want to minister to people in Hollywood," Amelia said simply. "I think God's calling me to it."

"Just don't get your hopes up," Sara cautioned.

Of course not all of Amelia's dreams came true. For years she prayed for a life partner and wrestled with her singleness. One of her favorite books on singleness was called, *"If I'm Waiting on God, Then What Am I Doing in a Christian Chatroom?"* by Christian comedian Kerri Pomarolli. Amelia enjoyed it so much she sent Kerri an email. To her surprise, Kerri responded, and the two became virtual friends.

When Amelia graduated from college, Kerri offered her an internship that introduced Amelia to the world of clean comedy. Amelia began to make connections, and eventually landed a job as a booking agent for comedians. She had to fly frequently for work. Guess where?

Sara still remembers the day she drove Amelia to the airport. She walked to the gate, hugged her daughter good-bye, and shook her head. "Well honey, I guess this just goes to show you can't put God in a box. You're going to Hollywood!"

It's fitting that someone who grasped the power of laughter would spend her life working with comedians. Amelia treasured her career. Not only did she pour herself into her work, but she held on to this unexpected gift from God like a precious jewel, an emblem of his generosity toward her.

"There are so many things God has given me," Amelia told me once. And then she started to recount them, one by one. Truly this was one of Amelia's greatest secrets…learning to treasure the "ordinary" gifts of God as a catalyst for extraordinary joy and gratitude. Ultimately, her delight was never in the gift so much as the Giver. She had His attention, affection, communion, and friendship. And that's why Amelia laughed. Many times over the phone she would tell me about some terrible ailment she faced, and then laugh out loud. Sometimes it bubbled up out of nowhere, and other times it was a hard-won choice.

There was a season when doctors actually thought her joy was a form of denial. Her attitude was so counter-cultural that they couldn't fathom someone in her condition having a light-hearted disposition.

"My mom corrected them," Amelia told me. "Because truly I'm not in denial. I know I'm going to die," she said. "I'm just not going to live like I'm dead while I'm still alive."

SOME DAYS YOU JUST HAVE TO LAUGH

Yesterday morning, my friend Josie called me. Josie and I met when we were at Columbia International University and both lived in the same dorm hall (shout out to all the Walker One dorm ladies!) I truly believe she was one of the greatest gifts God gave me while there, and we have been best buds ever since. Jo and I relate on a level that no one else understands because we both have physical disabilities. We're able to call each other, share our stories and frustrations, and laugh about our daily struggles because we both totally "get" it.

Yesterday was one of those days. Jo called and I answered and she said something like, "So dude, this morning at the track while exercising, my wheelchair flipped back and I hit my head and instantly thought of you." We both started laughing. Once we calmed down I said something like, "Yeah, I've hit my head so many times I have become an expert. So now when I fall, as I am going down I think of my head and try not to hit it, and about protecting any electronic devices I am carrying, namely my phone." (Priorities, people, priorities!) I then tell her that I have a recent fall story too.

This past Saturday my parents and I went to see the movie "Woodlawn." I was not feeling the greatest and in all honesty was a bit annoyed and not in the best of moods before walking out the door. As I was leaving, I got my purse and headed for the door to get my crutches and lost my balance, fell forward, and face planted into the dog bowls by the door. This was a lovely indication as to how my day was going so far. As soon as I hit the ground I started laughing so hard it made it impossible to get up and meanwhile my mom is nearby laughing too and neither one of us were much help to each other. Oh the joys of having Cerebral Palsy! But the truth is, it was totally what I needed to lighten my mood, and ironically it made the day a bit better.

I don't know what you are going through today, but I do know it's better to laugh than to cry. Enduring the hard days is so much easier if you can learn not to take everything so seriously. Laughter and friendship make everything a little better.

3AM WAKE-UP CALLS

In the past few weeks I have not slept well, having been woken up for one reason or another. Yesterday morning was no different. I woke up at 3am with some major issues with my colostomy bag. More crap to clean up—ha! There is no sweeter wake-up call than that (sigh). I definitely relate to all you moms out there who get very little sleep. It is a struggle for sure.

I got frustrated at first because of the mess and because I knew that sleep would not return easily. But then I remembered yesterday's post about not taking everything so seriously, so I tried to find the amusement in a very annoying situation. Sleep did not return until about 6am and even then I did not sleep long.

However, the positive in this situation is that I was able to read some very encouraging devotions during that time and to pray. I have been reminded that these unexpected wake-up calls provide an excellent time to pour out my heart to the Lord and to ponder His Word. He always manages to help me put things into perspective and finds some way to get through to my sleep-deprived brain. So the next time you find yourself unable to sleep, spend that time talking with God. I can assure you He will not disappoint, and He will give you the inner peace and rest your soul so desperately needs.

PEOPLE WHO INSPIRE: JONI EARECKSON TADA

When days are hard and life feels miserable, it's so easy to focus on ourselves and our problems. However, for me, that only leads to more despair. One practice that helps me look up and be encouraged on the hard days is reading inspiring testimonies from other believers. In particular the testimony of Joni Eareckson Tada has had a great impact on my life. Joni's life has not always been easy, but she has dealt with her trials with Christ-like joy and allowed God to be glorified through her difficulties.

A couple of years ago, Joni spoke at an event with the comedian I managed at the time, and I was able to be there and meet her. What an honor and privilege! She is such a lovely lady and reading back through her story over the past few days has encouraged me to press on. If you've never read her autobiography, here's a brief review I wrote a few years ago to whet your appetite!

JONI: An Unforgettable Story is the touching autobiography of a woman who became a paraplegic at the age of eighteen, and since then has overcome tremendous obstacles in her life to become the woman she is today. In the first few chapters Joni educates the reader on her interests and hobbies from painting to riding horses.

However, not too long into the story, she takes the reader inside of what we know is coming: the diving accident that changed her life forever. Joni describes her journey of learning to live life as a paraplegic. She gives readers an authentic inside-peek into her most bitter and most joyful moments. Even though Joni went through a period of time where all she wanted to do was give up and die, she eventually realized that she could still have a meaningful life with a disability. She realized God could use her trials to glorify Himself and to help others.

Joni began painting again, but instead of using her hands, she drew with her teeth to create masterpieces. Her unique paintings became popular and have provided opportunities for Joni to share her story with the world, including being interviewed by Barbara Walters on *The Today Show*. Joni also founded a Christian-based organization called Joni and Friends, which provides assistance to disabled people all over the world.

Joni writes with such raw vulnerability that readers feel like they are right there with her experiencing everything. I found myself laughing through one sentence and crying through the next. At the end of her book, I was blessed by her testimony. I was reminded that God is not limited by our limitations, and that He can use them for His glory and our good.

This is the first of many books that Joni has authored. I recommend you read this as well as her others. Her books are excellent resources for people who are dealing with a disability or chronic illness. They will leave you encouraged and challenge you to grow in your own relationship with Christ.

IT'S SIMPLY TUESDAY

For most, Tuesday is just another day of the week. Boring. Uneventful. But it is yet another day to be grateful. This morning I go into the hospital for a small procedure that is not very fun. However, in the midst of the mundane and hard, there is joy to be found.

This past weekend my family and I spent the day on Lake Norman. We went on a lunch cruise around the lake and then met up with some friends who have a place there. It was such a wonderful family day and brought much joy to my heart. Also, being out and about again gave me glimmers of hope that my body is indeed continuing to heal. I praise the Lord for that. Sometimes it's the simplest things that bring the most joy. I am so thankful for the family God has blessed me with and the time God has allowed us to spend together. I'm thankful that they walk with me through the good and the bad. On this Tuesday, what are the joys in your life? Trust me, they are there, so take time to look for the joys God has given you today and be thankful.

PITY INTO PRAISE

In the past few weeks I have not slept well, waking up frequently for one reason or another. Most recently I haven't slept because of severe pain and nausea—side effects from treatments, which make me frustrated. Then I had a come-to-Jesus meeting that put my pity party in its place. I'm sure in your own struggles you know exactly what I mean. The Lord helped me find praise instead of pity. I promise that in the bleakest of times, if you stop and ask God to sprinkle some praise into your situation, He will.

~

God may not change your circumstance, but He can

certainly change your perspective.

~

God may not change your circumstance, but He can certainly change your perspective. That being said, during my sleepless nights I have tried to find joy instead of lamenting about how hard things are.

A couple activities that are helping me keep the right attitude during these long nights are praying and reading biographies from some of my heroes in the faith. The Lord has shown me that these unexpected wake-up calls provide an excellent time to pour out my heart to the Lord and to ponder His Word. It has also helped as I've read the stories of many others who have gone before me, such as Elisabeth Elliot, Amy Carmichael, and Darlene Rose, to name a few. The same God who walked them through their fires can carry me as well. I'm not the only one facing a trial, and I won't be the last one, so it's comforting to know I'm not alone.

The next time you find yourself unable to sleep, spend time talking to God. Ask Him to turn your pity into praise. I promise, He never disappoints.

KISS THE BANANA CAKE GOOD-BYE

I love cake, especially my mom's cake. My mom makes the best cakes in the world! (I am not biased or anything). However, since my surgery I've had to change many things about my lifestyle, including my diet. Before my surgery I read and researched eating plans from others who had undergone the same procedure. Some said their diet changed tremendously, while others said that after a month or so they were able to resume a normal, well-balanced diet. I was optimistic that I would fall into the latter category. Unfortunately, that did not occur.

Much to my dismay, my digestive system has decided to rebel on me and not cooperate with anything other than cheese, eggs, a bit of bread, baked potatoes, chicken, tuna, and very mild spices. Pretty much everything has to be bland, bland, bland. This has been death to my flavor-loving palate and sweet tooth. My body will not tolerate any vegetables—cooked or raw—most fruits, steak, nuts, coconut, popcorn, most desserts, and the list goes on.

That being said, this past weekend our church was having a barbecue and my mom made cakes for it. One of those cakes happened to be my favorite—BANANA! I can eat a banana on occasion so I just knew I could splurge and have some cake. For health reasons, I had not had this cake in over a year so I was in cake heaven. I had a piece on Saturday and a very small piece on Sunday along with a barbecue sandwich. All was going well, or so I thought, until Monday evening. Let the pain and nausea party begin! It lasted for two days, carrying over into yesterday as well. So much for my optimism that "a little bit won't hurt." Yeah right!

So along with the many other things I have kissed goodbye this year, the time has come for me to kiss my sweet banana cake goodbye. No more for me. I know I sound a bit dramatic—after all it is just food—but adjusting to this new diet and way of life over the past six months has been hard. However, the Lord so sweetly reminded me yesterday to get over myself and my wants, and to remember that He has provided me with what I need to live. These foods I so greatly desire, are not necessary for my survival. I was reminded to be thankful for this season even though it does not include many of the things I was once able to enjoy.

The stripping-away process is never easy, but it's necessary for our growth. I will leave you with the passage below, and I hope God uses it to encourage your soul today, as it did mine:

> Therefore I tell you, do not worry about your
> life, what you will eat or drink; or about your
> body, what you will wear. Is not life more than
> food, and the body more than clothes? Look
> at the birds of the air; they do not sow or reap

or store away in barns, and yet your heavenly Father feeds them. Are you not much more valuable than they? Can any one of you by worrying add a single hour to your life? (Matthew 6:25-27).

PURITY OF MIND

"Finally, brothers and sisters, whatever is true, whatever is noble, whatever is right, whatever is pure, whatever is lovely, whatever is admirable—if anything is excellent or praiseworthy—think about such things. Whatever you have learned or received or heard from me, or seen in me—put it into practice. And the God of peace will be with you" (Philippians 4:8).

One thing God has been challenging me with lately is purity of mind. As Christians we should regularly evaluate the purity of our thoughts. By default, it's easy to allow our minds to be filled with worry, stress, anger, bitterness, jealousy, and so much more. At times we may wonder why we can't get such thoughts from our minds, or why we can't feel God's presence. However, if we are feeding our minds with things of this world, we're bound to reap the consequences.

In the early years of my parent's marriage, my dad worked the night shift. My mom was alone in the evenings and often felt afraid. However, one night in particular she was more fearful than normal. She prayed for the Lord to take her fear away, and to remove the feeling of darkness that was around her. She had been watching a television show and immediately felt the Lord tell her "Sara, how can I take this fear away, when you are feeding it with what you are watching?" From that point forward my mom was more selective regarding the things she watched, read, and listened to.

I was reminded of this recently, and realized that I have let my guard down in this area more than I should have. Below are some questions that I ask myself regarding these areas, and I thought I would share them with you:

1. Are the television shows and movies I am watching glorifying to the Lord? How do I feel once I've watched it? Does it make me have sinful thoughts or attitudes?
2. Does the music I listen to glorify the Lord? Does it cause me to want to draw closer to Him or does it make me discontent?
3. Do the books and magazines I read glorify the Lord or do they bring negative thoughts to my mind?
4. Do the conversations I engage in glorify the Lord or myself? Do the words I use affirm others or tear them down?

Here are some Bible verses to ponder:

Romans 12:2: "Do not conform any longer to the pattern of this world, but be transformed by the renewing of your mind. Then you will be able to test and approve what God's will is–his good, pleasing and perfect will."

Proverbs 4:23: "Keep your heart with all vigilance, for from it flow the springs of life."

Ephesians 4:22-24: "To put off your old self, which belongs to your former manner of life and is corrupt through deceitful desires, and to be renewed in the spirit of your minds, and to put on the new self, created after the likeness of God in true righteousness and holiness."

As you go throughout your week, ask God to show you what habits you need to eliminate or change. Focus on the verses above and commit them to memory as they will help center your mind and heart on the right things. Praying for you all.

BUT FIRST, JESUS

I can't believe spring is already around the corner. As I think of spring I pray for fresh ideas and new beginnings. With those, come prayers for my health as well. The past few weeks have been especially hard dealing with lots of pain and nausea from these bladder infections. I have pretty much been completely bed-bound. However, the Lord has been extremely gracious on the hard days, reminding me of different reasons to have joy. One Bible verse that keeps coming to my mind recently is Nehemiah 8:10. It says, "This day is holy to our Lord. Do not grieve, for the joy of the Lord is your strength."

I love the book of Nehemiah. It's one of my favorite books of the Bible. Nehemiah was faced with much adversity, but with the help of the Lord, he did not let that stop him from being obedient to God's calling. Nehemiah faced a great deal of sadness, but he immediately took his worries and cares to the Father, crying out for His help and deliverance. Even though times were tough, God gave Nehemiah the strength he needed to press on, and proved that joy is not dependent upon circumstances. I am grateful for the nuggets of wisdom God has given me while studying this book.

Just like Nehemiah, I am facing a season of adversity. In my flesh I often feel like complaining to those around me and having a pity party. But first and foremost, I must take every thought and concern directly to the throne of the Almighty. There is no need to cry out to everyone else and ignore the Lord. He asks that we come to Him first for everything that we need. Nehemiah practiced this in his day-to-day life, and God never let him down.

MY TERRIBLE WEEK

You know how you have ideas of how a day or a week is going to go, and then everything falls apart and nothing goes as imagined? Say hello to my week! On Tuesday, I was all excited about the rest of the week because I was going to wake up early every day and have a nice long quiet time, then get lots of writing done. Guess what? It went nothing like that. When you have health problems sometimes they override the best of plans.

Tuesday morning started out so insane. First, I overslept. Then I woke up to discover a major disaster with my ileostomy bag— it was, quite literally, a crappy morning. This little episode took a while to clean up. After that I dropped my phone and ruined my phone case. Thankfully, the phone survived the drama, but a new phone case will be on order soon. And all of this happened BEFORE I had my coffee. That tells you how the rest of the day went.

Wednesday morning at 3:00am I woke up with severe bladder spasms and had issues all day that confined me to my bed with plenty of medicine. As a result I had to cancel appointments and plans for the day. Thursday was similar, and my mom and I were leaving to go out of town on Friday. Naturally, I was a bit frustrated and overwhelmed as I thought about everything I needed to get done and worried about how my health would hold up.

That's when the Lord so sweetly reminded me of truth from His Word in 2 Corinthians 12:9. "My grace is sufficient for you, for my power is made perfect in weakness. Therefore I will boast all the more gladly about my weaknesses, so that Christ's power may rest on me."

So things didn't go according to plan. Guess what? In the end, it was still okay and I got to rest in God's amazing grace. He has control of everything and in our weakness He is strong. Today, if you feel overwhelmed with everything on your plate, take a moment to stop and pray. Rest in the grace and strength that God so freely gives. I promise, going to Him is the key to a whole new perspective.

BEING THANKFUL DURING TRIALS

"I thank God for my handicaps for through them I have found myself, my work, and my God." This quote by Helen Keller always inspires me. Every time I read it, I am reminded that God uses our so-called "handicaps"—whatever they may be—to mature us and grow us closer to Him. Helen was a remarkable woman who did not let her struggles of being blind and deaf define her life. Instead of drowning in self-pity she allowed her disability to make her stronger, and it became a blessing rather than a curse.

I can relate to this in my own life. Growing up with CP, I have dealt with numerous challenges throughout my life, and recently been reminded of those challenges more than ever. However, as I look back on the struggles I have had, I am thankful for them because they have helped mold me into the woman I am today. Even though my life has been hard at times, it has been during those struggles that I have truly matured and most importantly grown closer to Jesus! Some of my biggest revelations in life have come in part to the struggles I have dealt with. Do I believe that Jesus rejoices in the suffering of His children? No, but I do believe that He will work everything out for His good, and will use our experiences to glorify Himself (Romans 8:28).

We all have our own set of "handicaps" we struggle with, and it is often hard to have a good perspective. Recently, that has been difficult for me. However, the Lord has reminded me of His faithfulness throughout my entire life, and no matter what He allows in this life I can find joy because He is my Savior. It is not about me and my desires, but about Him and His. The moment we drop the selfish attitude is the moment we start to learn from what He is doing. No matter what struggle you are facing right now, be encouraged that God does love you and wants to work in you. He

~

The moment we drop the selfish attitude is the moment we start to learn from what He is doing.

~

can make something good come out of the crappiest day. So just like our friend Helen Keller, take some time to thank God for your handicaps, for through them you have the potential to find yourself, your work, and your God.

SET YOUR MIND ON THINGS ABOVE

"Set your mind on things above, not on earthly things" (Colossians 3:2). So much of a person's joy and contentment comes from our perspective. It all comes down to what we are feeding our minds each day. For example, are your days spent fretting over the "what ifs" of life, or are you surrendering those thoughts to the Lord? Are you watching, reading, or listening to anything that triggers discontentment or envy? It is easy to allow our minds to be filled with worry, stress, anger, and fear, especially during difficult seasons. At times we may wonder why we can't get certain thoughts out of our heads, or why we cannot feel God's presence in a situation. However, if we are dwelling on the things of this world, those thoughts can produce in us discontentment, fear, and worry.

I love HGTV shows like "Fixer Upper" and "Rehab Addict." In and of themselves they are not bad and may seem harmless. But if watching them stirs discontentment or envy within your heart, you may need to reevaluate your viewing habits. Perhaps you don't wrestle with discontentment so much as fear—are you watching shows that feed the fearful thoughts in your mind? Are you reading books that keep your mind in a constant state of anxiety?

Then of course there's social media. It is so easy to scroll through Facebook or Pinterest and begin comparing yourselves to others. These social media outlets tend to help folks make life look picture-perfect, but nobody's life is perfect. When it seems like others have the perfect house, the perfect health, a wonderful husband, etc., it can trigger discouraging thoughts and feelings in our hearts before we even know what hit us. These outlets are not inherently bad, but if we allow them to grow seeds of jealousy, discontentment, and bitterness, then it is time to take a step back from them.

Being homebound and bed-bound leaves a lot of time for me to dwell on life and thoughts like never before. Some days I do not even leave my bedroom and my "view" is not very exciting. Because of this, I try to be guarded in how I fill my mind. Life is hard and dealing with a chronic illness every day is not easy. I learned a long time ago that in order to have the right mindset during these circumstances, I need to be guarded with how I spend my time, especially in regard to what I watch, read, and listen to. I am sick enough without stacking on worries, discontentment, and jealousy. My days and my suffering are so much easier to deal with when I am focusing on "things above," and not on my current circumstances.

HAPPY IN THE LORD

A recent apology to my mom, and a Joni Eareckson Tada devotional convicted me that I have lost my spirit of gratitude in the midst of a trial. In her devotional, Joni made a point that we always say we are thankful for God's strength through a circumstance, but we are never actually thankful for the circumstance or affliction itself.

Lately I have been dealing with continued health problems that I cannot control. However, I can control my attitude, which is something I have fallen short of lately, and for that I am sorry. I want a consistent, healthy, happy life, but the one thing I am not consistent in lately is reading the Word of God. No wonder I do not have a spirit of gratitude and no sense of peace.

1 Thessalonians 5:18 says to be "thankful in ALL circumstances." "All" does not mean only when things are going my way, when I have everything I want, or when I am in good health. No, it means in *everything*. How do we cultivate joyful gratitude in everything? Recently I was looking through some of my old writings, and found this quote from George Mueller:

I saw more clearly than ever, that the first great and primary business to which I ought to attend every day was, to have my soul happy in the Lord. The first thing to be concerned about was not, how much I might serve the Lord, how I might glorify the Lord; but how I might get my soul into a happy state, and how *my* inner man might be nourished.[6]

The Lord has been reminding me more than ever of the importance of spending time reading and absorbing His Word every day. It is so easy to get bogged down with the trials of life and neglect spending time with the Lord. However, that should be our most important priority before anything else.

True contentment and peace comes from spending time with Jesus. No matter where your discontentment lies—whether it be your health, singleness, job, or something else—you can find true joy and happiness by giving your time to Jesus. I do not know what you are struggling with today, but make it a priority to take some time to make your soul "happy in the Lord."

---

[6] George Mueller, *A Narrative of Some of the Lord's Dealing with George Muller, Written by Himself,* Jehovah Magnified. Addresses by George Muller Complete and Unabridged, 2 vols. (Muskegon, Mich.: Dust and Ashes, 2003), 2:730-731.

THE STRUGGLE IS REAL

It's been one of those Thursdays —actually make that, one of those *weeks!* As the popular phrase goes, "the struggle is real." That should be the theme of my life these days. Recently I read Psalm 128:24 which states, "This is the day the Lord has made, let us rejoice and be glad in it."

However, we all have days when we don't feel like rejoicing, and that has been me this week. I have slept and felt woozy for the last few days because of a new medication. On Monday I started taking a muscle relaxer for my spasticity. I've always had problems with that, but it has been worse since I have been sick this past year. Spasticity makes my muscles extremely tight and painful, and lately I have not been able to relax or sleep well because of it. Thankfully, during my Monday visit with a urologist, she noticed how severe it is and is referring me to a new neurologist. In the meantime, she gave me a muscle relaxer that is supposed to work well with CP. It is working, but it's also making me sleep a lot and I feel like a zombie… ha!

Although today I realized that the medicine has helped, and for now the side effects are worth it. I had been praying for less pain and more sleep and God has answered those prayers so instead of complaining about the negative aspects, I was convicted that I need to be thankful. It has brought much pain relief for me and I'm truly grateful for that. Praise Jesus. Hopefully as I continue to take it the side effects will lessen, but for now I'm glad for the ways it is helping. Thanks again for all of your thoughts, prayers, and encouraging words. God uses them to fill my days with joy!

THE JOY OF JESUS

Joy. Lately I've been praying for joy and peace. Lots of it. This past week has been rough health-wise. However, over the last few days I have been reminded yet again that joy is always ours for the taking. Life does not have to be perfect to be joyful, and health does not have to be good. In fact, joy is more precious when born out of difficulties.

Philippians 4:4 states, "Rejoice in the Lord always, again I say rejoice." Note, that this verse does not tell us to only be joyful in the good times but to be joyful *always*, no matter what comes our way. All of us have been through seasons where certain struggles threaten to steal our joy—the mundanity of life, the loneliness of singleness, the heartache of a difficult marriage, or the suffering of illness. Truthfully, some days are just plain crappy. Thankfully though, we have the Word of God to lead and guide us into the joy of Christ each and every day, regardless of the situations we face.

Paul is an excellent example in Scripture of a person who displayed joy in good and difficult times. He experienced many hardships and sufferings while following Christ, and Scripture tells us that he dealt with a "thorn in the flesh," but through it all he remained joyful. Paul tells the secret to this joy and contentment in a letter he wrote to the church of Philippi. Philippians 4:11-13 says:

> I am not saying this because I am in need, for I have learned to be content in whatever the circumstances. I know what it is to be in need, and I know what it is to have plenty. I have learned the secret of being content in any and every situation, whether fed or hungry, whether in plenty or in want. I can do all things through him who gives me strength.

With Christ, we can endure anything because of His strength —a strength that promises to sustain us. No matter what is going on in and around you, you can still have joy even in the worst of times. In fact, that's when Christ's supernatural joy can shine the most. It's easy to be selfish and get caught up with what we want. It's also easy to think that a joyful life is defined by a series of good moments and fulfilled desires. However, life is really defined by the work Jesus Christ is doing in you, and how He allows the "not so good moments" to mature you. I want to encourage you today to fight for joy. Be thankful for what God has given you. Spend time reading His Word daily. Ask Him to give you His never-ending joy. Follow His command to rejoice always! Be encouraged that in His presence there is fullness of joy (Psalm 16:11), and remember that God works out ALL things for the good of those who love Him (Romans 8:28).

The joy that comes in the morning after a long weary night is one of the best gifts Jesus offers us. In the darkest of days when joy seems impossible all we have to do is ask, and the Lord will meet us

~

It's easy to think that a joyful life is defined by a series of good moments and fulfilled desires. However, life is really defined by the work Jesus Christ is doing in you, and how He allows the "not so good moments" to mature you.

~

where we are. Our problems may not be resolved, but before long our heart doesn't seem as heavy nor our outlook as bleak. This is all because of a Savior who loves us with an everlasting love and delights in offering us His joy. Friend, I don't know what you are facing today but my prayer is that you will enter into the joy of the Lord. It is truly the best place to be.

LAUGHTER AND GRACE

Happy Monday, friends! I hope you all had a great weekend! Mine was incredibly blessed and full of laughter and grace. I am so thankful that in the midst of difficulty God provides encouraging and fun moments that uplift the soul—and that is exactly what He did for me this week.

On Wednesday one of my dearest friends, Casey, and her son Malakai came over for a visit. Then on Thursday morning I was able to Skype with my friend Erin, and that afternoon my friend Anita came over. We talked and laughed for the longest time and played with her new jewelry. What girl doesn't like to do that? On Saturday my aunt visited and brought her sweet granddaughter Lexi to visit, so of course I loved "Mimi time" with her.

On Saturday evening my church had a "Parade of Tables" event where ladies from the church decorate tables and each one has a different theme. Everyone joins together for dinner and entertainment, and this year the speaker was Cherie Nettles. Ya'll she was AMAZING! She is hilarious and now on the list of one of my favorite comedians. She also has a powerful testimony about the healing and grace God has brought into her life. Her talk reminded me of Jeremiah 32:17, which says, "Nothing is too hard for God."

As you go throughout your week, remember this truth from scripture: Nothing is too hard for God. Nothing. That sickness you want healed, the job you want, the husband or wife you wish for, the baby you want to have…the list could go on. God knows the mountain you are facing, and He also knows the desires of your heart. He knows and He cares even when it seems like He is absent from the circumstances. He is not absent. He is there and He is working even when we cannot see or feel evidence of Him.

In those moments we have to trust what we know of our Savior, and as Elisabeth Elliot says, "Do the next thing." When life is too hard and we do not know where to turn next, just do the next thing. Trust Jesus and do the next thing, and somewhere along the way you will begin to feel okay, and little by little you will sense His presence again, because actually He has never left.

HOPE A LITTLE MORE

"Above all there is this, look at Calvary. Look steadfastly. Take time to look and all within you will be hushed. For power streams forth from Calvary. We never need to know defeat."

~Amy Carmichael

WHEN AMELIA HOPED

The last time I spoke with Amelia, I could barely understand her. I strained through the familiar cadence of her voice to make out individual words. Her speech was weak and heavily slurred. Sara said that in the final weeks of her life, Amelia grew increasingly silent. On Tuesday morning, July 3, 2018, she woke in a panic. "I'm dizzy," she slurred. "Sit me up! Sit me up! I'm so dizzy."

She hadn't been able to sit up for the past eight months, so Sara knew she was disoriented. They calmed her down, but from then on Amelia rarely opened her eyes because it was too hard to focus on anything. On Saturday, July 8, I sent Amelia a text to see how she was doing. Her mom responded:

> Hey Jeanne, this is Amelia's mom. Amelia had a major decline on Thursday. Unless God performs a miracle, Amelia is soon to meet Jesus face to face. Pray for us all. Amelia loved you lots. Sara

Sobs caught in my chest. I knew this was coming, but it felt too soon. I dialed their home number and Sara answered. It was the first time we ever spoke on the phone, but it felt as though we'd known each other forever. We were connected through one extraordinary person. As we talked on the phone, Sara told me that earlier that afternoon they had witnessed a precious moment. It was a story I'll never forget.

One of Amelia's friends was pregnant with a little girl, soon to be named Jubilee Amelia. Amelia very much wanted to meet the baby—her namesake—before she passed. When Sara heard baby Jubilee had arrived, she sent word that Amelia had taken a turn for the worse. "We'll be there right away," Jubilee's parents said. That very afternoon, they placed the newborn baby in Amelia's arms. Jubilee Amelia—a tiny taste of her legacy in the most precious form. Amelia could scarcely talk nor see. But they said tears streamed down her face as she held the baby.

"I wonder what she was thinking," Sara mused as we spoke on the phone.

Later as I thought about the story, I remembered a conversation Amelia and I once had regarding her singleness. She said there was a season when she struggled deeply with the fact that God had not given her a life partner, or even a boyfriend.

"I couldn't understand why God wouldn't give me just a glimpse of that experience," she said. "Then one day, it hit me. He protected me. He knew that eventually I'd be completely bed-bound. All I have is time. I could lie in bed all day long and agonize over why some guy left me. Or what could have been, or how much I miss him. But I don't have any of that! I'm totally free from the wounds and scars of a failed relationship." And then she said something incredible: "Jeanne...Jesus is the only man I've ever loved! He's the love of my life!"

Amelia recognized the beauty and simplicity of singular devotion to Christ. She tasted the true gift of singleness. She went on, "Besides, there's so many things He's given me. I asked Him for a ministry in Hollywood, and God gave it to me. I asked Him for a platform to write, and He gave it to me..." She went on and on, marveling again and again, "He gave it to me."

I bet that as Amelia held that baby and tears streamed down her face, she was thinking, "He gave it to me." She asked God for this small gift—the chance to meet her namesake—and two days before she died, God gave it to her.

When Amelia hoped, big things happened. Strongholds of bitterness gave way to gratitude. Weakness became strength, and sorrow turned to joy. To the world these moments may seem inconsequential, but to Amelia they were the bedrocks of her faith. Proof of His love, goodness, and generosity.

It's a strange thing to walk with a friend through the transition from life to death. As I prayed for her constantly in the following days, I realized this was my final act of friendship. She had one last battle to fight, and then never again would I have the privilege of walking alongside her through life.

Months later when her mom called to talk about writing a book, and the project began to take shape, I found myself re-immersed in Amelia's final thoughts. In this last section, you'll see

Amelia's writing take a turn. As her illness progresses, the cry of her heart becomes simple and raw. Where she once hoped for healing, she begins to hope for nothing but Jesus.

Just Jesus.

The greatest hope of all.[7]

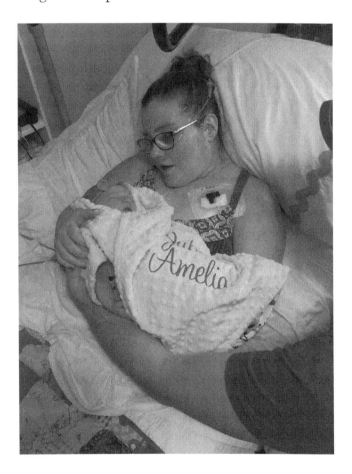

HOPE A LITTLE MORE

2014 has been an incredibly hard year. Depressing way to start a post, I know, but it's true. Over the past several years my health has been steadily declining, but for a long time I was not sure why. However in October I received some answers. Because of my CP, I have always had something called Neurogenic Bowel Syndrome. But recently I found out that my colon and intestines have completely shut down, which is why I am staying so sick. My situation is atypical due to previous surgeries I've had, which makes things a bit more complicated. It took a while to find a specialist qualified to treat my case. God finally provided a surgeon, and after many appointments and tests, I am now awaiting a surgery date which I hope will be sometime at the beginning of January.

Throughout the years I have had many health challenges, but I would say this has been the hardest. I've had to move in with my parents until I am better, take a leave of absence from my job, and basically become completely dependent. If you know me at all, you know that has not been easy. This sickness has emptied me of everything I have, and yet God is daily giving me the strength I need to make it. That has been so freeing. I am completely out of control and there is nothing I can do to change my circumstances, but I know the One who can. In the midst of my suffering I have grown closer to the Lord and I better understand Philippians 4:7, which talks about peace beyond understanding. I know that peace now.

There are so many unknowns as to what is ahead and questions such as, "Will the surgery be successful? Will healing come soon? How is all this going to turn out?" I do not have the answers, but God does and that is all that matters. After all, my life is not mine and there is nothing more freeing than handing my life and everything I have over to Jesus. That is the definition of true freedom. One of my goals for 2015 is to live in this freedom and be joyful no matter the circumstances. I am thankful daily for the hope of Christ, and as one of my favorite songs states, I will "dance a little, laugh a little, and hope a little more."

I would like to give a special thanks to my mom and dad. They have been amazing through this and take such good care of me. I couldn't do this without them. Also, to all my friends, thanks for being so gracious and encouraging. I know many of you have prayed for me over the past few months, and I greatly appreciate all the prayers. Let me know how I can be praying for you. I hope you all have a blessed new year and a wonderful 2015!

SUFFERING FOR HIS GLORY

At some point in life, everyone experiences suffering. During these times it's easy to wonder why God isn't delivering us as fast as we would like Him to. That's been my own question lately. I know God is powerful and He does not rejoice in my suffering, so why doesn't He choose to deliver me? Recently I read some passages of Scripture that reminded me of the answer to this question.

In John 11 Jesus' friend Lazarus is sick, and his sisters Mary and Martha call for Jesus to come. However, Jesus waits a few days before traveling to Bethany and by the time He reaches them, Lazarus is dead. The sisters greet Him with tremendous grief, wondering why He didn't come sooner. After all, He alone could have prevented their brother from dying! The disciples also question Jesus, but His response is, "Lazarus's sickness will not end in death. No, it happened for the glory of God so that the Son of God will receive glory from this" (John 11:4).

Did Jesus rejoice in the death of His friend? No, He did not. In fact, this passage tells us that Jesus wept over Lazarus's death. But He allowed it because in the end it would display the glory of God.

Another similar example can be found in John 9, which tells the story of a man born blind. In this passage the disciples ask Jesus who sinned that caused the man to be blind—the man or his parents. Jesus responds by saying, "'Neither this man or his parents sinned,' said Jesus, 'but this happened so that the works of God might be displayed in him'" (John 9:3).

When we undergo trials it's easy to think, "What have I done wrong to deserve this?" Yes, we live in a fallen world and sometimes our suffering is a direct result of our sin. But that's not always the case. Jesus Himself said that the blind man's suffering was not a result of his sin or his parents' sin. Rather God allowed him to be blind for many years so that the glory of God would be displayed in his life.

People often ask me why I believe God allowed me to be born with a physical disability. I will never fully know the answer to that question here on earth, but the one thing I do know is that "God works all things for the good of those who love Him and who are called according to His purpose" (Romans 8:28). Disability or not, as a Christian I have been called to a higher purpose and that is to serve Jesus Christ no matter my circumstances.

2 Corinthians 12:9 teaches that God works out His power in our weakness. When we are weak He is strong. I firmly believe that there are times when God shines the brightest in our weaknesses. If we were perfect and never had any trials, what need would we have for God? God can use what we deem "tragic" for His ultimate good.

No matter what suffering you face today, God sees you and knows what you are going through. He will always be your source of comfort. Allow your suffering—whatever it may be—to draw you closer to your Savior. May your ultimate goal be to glorify Him, no matter your circumstances.

UPDATE ON MY RECOVERY

As many of you know I had my colon removed on January 23 because my bowels had shut down. The past year has been extremely hard for me. I stayed super sick, and was looking forward to this surgery because I knew that after recovery I would start to feel better. Going into this I knew it was going to be tough, but I had no idea how hard things were actually going to be. I'm glad I was naive because if I had known everything that was going to happen I wouldn't have entered into this so easily.

Following surgery I stayed in the hospital for five days. However, things did not go well when I returned home. After being home for one day I became extremely sick and had to go back to the hospital where I was told that my intestines had not woken up. Nothing was working. This was the start of some long and difficult weeks. During this time I was fighting for my life. There were several times when we thought I wouldn't make it, but the Lord's grace and strength kept me going. Two weeks into the hospital stay we thought things were improving, but then things took a turn for the worse. I started having terrible pain that I have never experienced before, and we soon found out that this pain was being caused by two blockages. On February 18, I had another surgery to remove the blockages and was told my small intestine was in the shape of a pretzel. Thankfully, following the second surgery I slowly began to improve, and was finally able to return home on March 3. That was such a beautiful day for me because for a while I thought I would never see home again.

This journey has humbled me in so many ways and made me completely depend on the Lord. He has revealed that His grace is always sufficient in weakness, and I am so thankful for that. This process has caused me to appreciate the life God has given me more than ever before, and to appreciate the little daily joys I am given.

Even though I am at home, I have a long road ahead with my recovery. I am still not able to stay by myself so I have to have someone stay with me and help me do everything. I am so thankful for the help that God has so graciously provided, and for my wonderful parents who have been with me through all of this and taken such great care of me. I am also thankful for Evelyn the sweet lady who stays with me during the week, and for the team of nurses that come weekly to help care for me. At first, it was hard for me to accept all of this help, but the Lord has used it to humble my heart and to help me draw nearer to Himself.

I want to thank all of my friends, family, church, and community who have prayed, visited, brought food and gifts, and provided encouragement for my family. I could never thank you all enough. We love you! I look forward to what God has ahead for me, and I will update again soon!

BE ANXIOUS FOR NOTHING

"Cast your anxiety on Him because He cares for you" (1 Peter 5:7). This verse has been coming to my mind over and over again lately. I was up all night on Friday, sick from pain and nausea, and my pain worsened throughout the day yesterday. Last night my heart rate was dangerously high so I went to the ER. I've always had a high heart rate but never this severe. Thankfully after several large doses of meds and antibiotics, it finally slowed down. Also, while there, the doctor read my urine culture from last week and it confirmed an infection. I could not have asked for better service in the ER. Everyone was extremely nice and helpful. I'm super grateful for my parents and my cousin Laurie who went with me last night. So thankful for all they do for me.

The infection and pain are the causes of my high heart rate. However, they did a couple tests to make sure my heart was okay and praise the Lord, all turned out good. I'm still planning to go to Winston Salem tomorrow for my appointment with a urology specialist, but we are waiting to drive down in the morning, and not today as originally planned. All of that being said, I woke this morning feeling very overwhelmed, but that is when the Lord reminded me of this verse in 1 Peter.

So often, instead of giving our cares to Jesus, we share them with everyone else. I have a tendency to be anxious and worry. My mom has often told me that as soon as I drop one worry, I pick up another. However, that is not how God wants us to live. Throughout Scripture He makes it very clear that we should be anxious for nothing, and an example of this is found in Philippians 4:6-7. I like the way *The Message* paraphrases it:

> Don't fret or worry. Instead of worrying, pray. Let petitions and praises shape your worries into prayers, letting God know your concerns. Before you know it, a sense of God's wholeness, everything coming together for good, will come and settle you down. It's wonderful what happens when Christ displaces worry at the center of your life.

Jesus does not find joy in seeing His children fret and suffer. He does not promise a life free of pain, but He does promise to comfort us and give us what we need. He delights, pursues relentlessly, and desires to give us rest. As we surrender and submit to Him, our entire perspective changes. Being physically sick is hard enough without adding worry into the mix. Even though the past few days have not been easy for me, Jesus has given me the joy and grace I need for each moment, which makes my sickness seem more tolerable. As a follower of Christ, He is my first love and the King of my heart. Instead of limiting us, submitting to Christ frees us to be the people He created us to be.

~

Instead of limiting us, submitting to Christ frees us to be the people He created us to be.

~

Whether you are going through a season of joy or sorrow, I hope these nuggets of truth will encourage you as they have me this morning. Thank You Jesus for comforting my soul today and for giving me peace and a reason to praise even in the storm! That is my prayer for each of you as well.

REST

This past week has been a hard one. My body is struggling with infections. I have been dealing with staph/skin infections and now a sore throat. Yesterday was spent in bed, and today will be much of the same. My body is in total rebellion at the moment. Earlier as I was thinking about everything and feeling overwhelmed, God gently reminded me of the verse in Matthew 11:28-30 that states, "Come to me, all you who are weary and burdened, and I will give you rest. Take my yoke upon you and learn from me, for I am gentle and humble in heart, and you will find rest for your souls. For my yoke is easy and my burden is light."

In the quiet of yesterday afternoon I was reminded that even in the hardest circumstances I can always be at rest, and the reason for that is Jesus. Jesus will carry my burdens so I do not have to. He loves me and desires to give me freedom. God does not intend for any of us to live as overwhelmed, anxious, or tired souls when He offers His rest. This does not mean God will never allow us to have trouble, but that He will carry us through our troubles with sustaining strength and grace.

Sickness may be present, jobs may be lost, marriages may fail, discontentment may abound, but Jesus wants us to let go of these stresses and come to Him. He is ready. He is waiting. He will fight your giants, if you will let Him. I am so guilty of striving and wanting to do more, more, and more. However, God has shown me lately that it is not how much I can do for Him, but instead how much I rest in Him.

He wants all of me; He wants to be the King of my heart in both the good and hard times. He wants my trust in every area of life, including the trials. Rest can only come when you are fully surrendered to Christ, trusting Him to care for you in the way He feels is best, no matter the circumstances.

SOMEWHERE DOWN THE ROAD

Sometimes life can just be plain hard. Sometimes answers do not come. Sometimes we wonder if they ever will. In these moments fear can take the place of peace in our hearts, and fear can rule in place of Jesus Christ. The older I get and the more I live, the more I am reminded that peace does not come from our possessions, relationships, health, or financial security.

No, true peace only comes from Jesus. Over the last year I feel that my life has been stripped away, and much like the changing of seasons, the Lord has been changing my life and maturing me into a stronger woman for Him. It seems like everything that I have put confidence in has been removed by God, but it has also drawn me closer to Him and shown me what is really important.

A life lived for God is not meant to be a life lived in ease. A life lived for God is meant to be a life surrendered to the Father, saying "not my will, but Yours be done." That also includes accepting and rejoicing in suffering. In the midst of trials and uncertainty, fear can tend to take over. However, God commands us throughout His word, "do not fear" and "do not be afraid" (Joshua 1:9). We may not know what is ahead, but He does. So in whatever you may be going through today, "Cast your cares on Him for he cares for you" (1 Peter 5:7). Surrender your life to Him—your struggles, your joys, everything. He is strong enough to handle them, so let Him. We may not understand all of God's plans on this side of Eternity but one day we will. As one of my favorite songs from Amy Grant says:

> *Somewhere down the road,*
> *There'll be answers to the questions.*
> *Somewhere down the road,*
> *Though we cannot see it now.*
> *Somewhere down the road,*
> *You will find mighty arms reaching for you.*
> *And they will hold the answers at the end of the road.*[8]

---

[8] Amy Grant. *Somewhere Down the Road.* Sparrow Records, 2010.

LEAVE IT IN THE HANDS OF THE HEALER

Tomorrow I go in for another surgery on my small bowel. Because of my previous surgeries, there could be a lot of risks involved with this. However, I am praying that all goes well and the surgery will improve my quality of life. The past few months have been extremely hard. I have spent a lot of time in bed with a lot of pain, but in the midst of it all God has been incredibly gracious. He has blessed me with two wonderful parents who love and care for me so well. I know it is not always easy for them, but they show Jesus to me every day in their care of me. God has also blessed me with an amazing group of friends who daily encourage me in different ways and are continually praying for me. It is so much easier going through hard seasons when you have a solid group of people alongside you. I thank God daily for the community He has given me.

Most importantly though, I thank God for the relationship I have with Jesus Christ. Without Jesus, I would be living as a lady with no hope. Without Jesus, I would be scared out of my mind right now. Without Jesus, I would be bitter. But with Jesus, I have LIFE and HOPE even on the most dreary days.

When my body is tired and overwhelmed and I don't know how to pray, the Lord knows. He understands and gives me the nudge I need to carry on. At times it may seem that the Lord is completely absent, but He is not. He is always there loving and leading. The Lord knows me better than anybody and loves me more than anyone ever could, so why do I doubt Him? Why do I fear? He has proven faithful over the course of my 31 years, and He will continue to be faithful.

Over the weekend, I let fear and worry creep in my mind. They brought along misery, sadness, anger, and doubt. During those moments the Lord gently reminded me that since I have Him, I should have no fear. This verse came to mind from Isaiah 41:10, "So do not fear, for I am with you; do not be dismayed, for I am your God. I will strengthen you and help you; I will uphold you with my righteous right hand." This truth from Scripture reminded me that I have no reason to worry. God wants to know that I trust Him and will surrender my everything to Him even if I don't know what the future holds.

My act of obedience during this season is trusting the Lord and fearing Him instead of fearing my circumstances. As tomorrow nears I am focusing on fearing God and trusting Him to carry me through. As one of my favorite songs says, "leave it in the hands of the Healer and walk away."

TRUSTING HIM IN THE ROAD AHEAD

"Trust in the Lord with all of your heart and lean not on your own understanding, but in all your ways acknowledge Him and He will direct your paths" (Proverbs 3:5-6). Trust is something we all struggle with from time to time. I know for me it is hard, especially when I do not know what lies ahead. I am a planner by nature, and I like to know exactly what is going on. However, God has reminded me lately to rest in Him and relinquish all my questions: "When will I get better?" "When will I be able to work again?" "When will God bring that future husband that I have prayed for, for years?"

~

The details of my future are not nearly as important as my daily trust and obedience.

~

As these questions have gone through my mind, God has reminded me of the past, and how through every season He has been faithful to guide me. The details of my future are not nearly as important as my daily trust and obedience. It is comforting to me during times of the unknown to know that Jesus loved me so much that He died on the cross so that I might have life. Trusting in that great love will never lead me astray, and that is the only consistent thing that brings peace in all of my uncertainty. I pray that wherever you are, you can trust God today with your uncertainties and that you can find the peace that comes from resting in Him.

HEALTH UPDATE

2015 has been quite the journey for me thus far. I turned 30 this year and I joked with someone the other day that I want a 30 do-over! Although since my last surgery in February, I have made some wonderful progress. Over the past couple of weeks, I have started getting out and doing more activities. I even made it to church. That was a huge blessing because I have been physically unable to go in so long. I realize these things are not major for most people, but for me they are. That being said, I have definitely been feeling hopeful about the days to come.

However, since this last surgery, I have been having problems with my bladder. I have had bladder issues for years, which have required multiple surgeries. Over the last few years things have been under control…until now. To make a really long story short, I have bladder problems stemming from my CP. When I was in 7th grade a surgeon completely rebuilt my bladder. Unfortunately my recent colon surgery, together with treatments and extended time in the hospital, has caused my bladder to shrink significantly. Hence my current bladder problems.

At this point the treatment for my situation consists of two things: botox in my bladder and eventually another major bladder surgery where my bladder will be removed. Depending on how the botox works, this surgery could occur one or three years from now. As you can imagine, this was not the news I was hoping to hear and in the moment I asked God, "What are you doing? I can't even begin to understand this. Can my body undergo yet another major surgery and be okay? What about my hopes and dreams? When can I get back to life as normal?"

But after much prayer, God reminded me not to worry about tomorrow and focus only on the things of today as He commands in Matthew 6:34. He has given me so much to be thankful for. He is continually restoring me. Yes, I may have major bladder surgery in my future, and it may come sooner than I would like. But if and when that day comes, God will be with me just as He always has. I am not being obedient to God and His Word by worrying about the what-ifs and creating scenarios of what might happen in my mind. That is me giving into my fears instead of turning them over to Christ.

Why is it that we make things harder on ourselves than they have to be, instead of letting the peace of Christ rule in our hearts? I want to encourage you with this truth today: no matter your worries, fears, or circumstances, Christ is strong enough to take care of them all. Give them over to Him, and let His strength carry you.

THE GREAT SURRENDER

The past couple of weeks have been some of the most difficult of my life. I am continually keeping a bladder infection, and the latest one landed me in the hospital by going sepsis. Sepsis has been a fear of mine since having these infections. I have continually prayed against that, but praise God it was caught in time and was treatable. However, I am still very weak, and it is likely that another infection will be returning soon.

At the beginning of my hospital stay I was very worried, and I'm still concerned. Although, after spending much time with the Lord, I have peace and my heart has a wonderful sense of freedom which only comes from Jesus. Worrying and fretting does not help my situation at all. The Lord has continually reminded me over the last several days of the tremendous weight that would be lifted off my shoulders by once again trusting Him. Why is it we tend to fight for control when Jesus says, "Let me carry this for you." This is where suffering and faith meet — believing Jesus when healing is not guaranteed, believing Jesus on the days where there are absolutely no answers, believing Jesus when I cannot get the quick appointment with one of the only specialists in the state that is experienced enough to take my case, and believing Jesus when the only plan of attack is to treat each infection as they come knowing they will continue to come one after the other because there is no permanent cure, and believing Jesus when there is no visible end in sight.

This is my life right now and these are the struggles I bring to Jesus every single day. Without Jesus these trials would make me want to curl up in a ball and never come out again, and it is because of Jesus that I can honestly say today that I am free. Of course each day is still hard and I have to surrender these things anew every morning, but God has met me every single time. If I believe that God is who He says He is, and I take the Bible at its Word, then even on the worst days, I can still be 100% free because I am in Christ. By taking my position in Christ, I can walk through whatever comes my way. He will give me strength for the trials and a sense of joy that only comes from a surrendered life.

~

If I believe that God is who He says He is, and I take the Bible at its word, then even on the worst days I can still be 100% free because I am in Christ.

~

I may not know what is ahead for my health tomorrow, but I am finding solace in trusting in the great Physician who does. I have never felt so out of control or as in the dark about where my life is headed, but there is also freedom in that. I don't need to worry about taking charge, or figuring out what is next because God has the ultimate control and there is nothing else I can do to change my circumstances. God only asks that I trust Him and allow Him to lead me.

Many of you have asked for a health update and I want to thank you for your continued thoughts and prayers. A few days ago I just finished a round of antibiotics and I am already having symptoms of the infection flaring up again. I had a test on Wednesday, but do not have the results yet. Unfortunately, I will not be able to see Dr. K (the urologist in Charlotte) until October even though many phone calls have been made. However, I do see his nurse practitioner in May. The plan for now is to continue to see my local doctor and my infectious disease doctors, and for them to treat my symptoms to the best of their knowledge. I do see my GP on Monday and then I see my ID the week after next. Today, I have been experiencing lots of pain and nausea so prayers for that to calm would be greatly appreciated. Also, prayers for wisdom for my local team of physicians would appreciated as well. I am humbled as to how many folks are praying for me. It means more than you will ever know.

I am going to try to post more frequently, and share what God is teaching me through this journey. While we are all facing different circumstances, I want my blog to be a place that will encourage you in whatever you may be walking through, and to remind you that you are not alone. My desire is for you to leave my blog encouraged by God's truth and His Word, and for it to be a place to cheer each other on.

HOPE A LITTLE MORE, PART 2

In 2014, I wrote a post titled "Hope a Little More," and now almost three years later it seems appropriate again. I wrote that post prior to a major surgery, shortly after discovering my colon had shut down. I honestly had no idea what to expect in the future. Fast forward two years later, and I am finding myself in the same boat, but instead of my colon it is now my bladder that is causing a lot of problems. I have been on antibiotics continually for almost a year now, and my infection went sepsis a month ago. I am now on super strong treatments over the next couple of months.

On Monday I went to   Charlotte to see my urologists's PA. Usually my time with her is not very productive and Monday's visit was typical. However, she did tell me that she thought my options were limited surgically, and that even if I had surgery my quality of life from these infections would not improve. She also mentioned two other small options for treatment, but those may not work either and I would have to wait for final decisions from the urologist. Unfortunately, I am not scheduled to see him until October and no matter how many times I have tried, they will not move up the appointment date. The conclusion for now is that nothing else can really be done except to treat the infection until it cannot be treated anymore.

The PA wants me to stay on my treatment plan with the Infectious Disease doctor and do what he says until I see the urologist in October. Even though my parents and I have discussed this scenario many times, it is still hard to hear. No matter how prepared you are, no one wants to hear that nothing else can be done.

I am a planner by nature and I like to have a plan and timeline, but I have no idea how long we can make the treatments work or when the infection will get bad again. I have been reminded this week more than ever that I'm not the one in charge of my life, plans, or desires; Jesus is. He alone knows what my future holds and my trust in Him is being pushed to another level.

My dear friend Kristin texted earlier this week and said that I was going to get to know God in a new and unique way through this. She also mentioned that this is the type of surrender and trust that only comes from a situation like this—one that is completely out of our hands. She is right, and even though this week has been hard, God has continued to carry me and give me hope with each new day.

One passage that has comforted me lately is Psalm 27:13-14, which says, "I would have despaired unless I had believed that I would see the goodness of the Lord in the land of the living. Wait for the Lord; be strong and let your heart take courage; yes, wait for the Lord." Moving forward I am going to find the good in each day and enjoy the little things God brings my way. I will also allow His courage to carry me, and most importantly I will not lose hope because of Jesus. He is HOPE, and it my privilege to serve Him all of my days.

Thanks to everyone for your prayers. Pray for my parents as they continue to care for me. I know it's not easy for them either so please pray for their encouragement. Also, pray that that we have peace beyond our understanding no matter the outcome, and that we are able to "hope a little more" each day.

THE END OF THE ROAD

One year ago today I was told news that changed my life forever. Over the past couple of years my health has been slowly declining, but in the summer of 2014 it took a turn for the worse. Last July I got really sick and stayed nauseated all of the time. A lot of days I could not even get out of bed. I went to my family physician and she ran a bunch of tests, one being a CT scan of my stomach. According to the radiology report, nothing major showed up in the scan except for gas. Fast forward to October 8, 2014, when I visited my urologist in Charlotte.

The day started out with a migraine, and I almost didn't go to the appointment because I felt terrible and figured that this visit would provide no new answers. It turns out I was very wrong. When the doctor came in, the first thing he said was, "What are we going to do?"

"I don't know," I replied.

To which he said, "We are at the end of the road."

I asked him what he meant by that, and he told me my colon had shut down and anything we did from this point forward would be "grasping at straws." I was stunned and confused as to how he knew this because he had not done any recent tests. It turns out he had viewed the CT scan from July, and it did indeed reveal more than just gas. He assumed I already knew this information, which was one of the reasons I was there.

My mom was with me that day, and we both sat there in a state of shock and confusion. We were in the office a couple more hours as they explained all of the options that could be next. They were talking about doctors I would need to see and complications that could occur. Because of surgeries I've had previously, and other health problems, finding a surgeon willing to treat my case and do surgery was going to be a difficult—if not impossible—task. But we know from Scripture that nothing is impossible with God. Even though I went home that day feeling more overwhelmed than I had ever felt before, God's peace surrounded me and carried me through what was going to be a very difficult road.

One year later, by God's miraculous healing and strength, after life threatening surgery and almost six weeks of being in the hospital—I am still alive and on the other side of this long journey. I am still in recovery mode but making progress each day and constantly reminded of God's amazing faithfulness. He is so good! For those of you who have been with me every step of the way in this, thank you so much for all of the prayers and support. It means more than you will ever know.

THE GOODNESS OF THE LORD

The past few weeks have been very hard, especially after being in the hospital for a complete bowel blockage. It is literally a miracle that I'm alive and that I'm writing this from home and not a hospital. However, the goodness of God has prevailed. One of my favorite verses right now states, "I would have despaired unless I had believed I would see the goodness of the Lord in the land of the living" (Psalm 27:13).

These days, it can be quite a challenge to find the good in my circumstances. Sometimes my flesh wants to scream out, "How can any good come from this?!" However, God has blown me away with His compassion and mercy. According to my doctors, I should still be in the hospital trying to survive from a complicated surgery. My doctor's exact words were, "If you don't have the surgery you will die, and even with surgery you might die." That overwhelmed my parents and I so much, but we prayed and called on all our prayer warriors. Praise God—surgery was not needed!

Also the Lord has allowed me to see and spend time with dear friends who I never get to see. Our fellowship and conversations may have taken place in a hospital room or in my hospital bed at home, but visiting with everyone was just the encouragement my weary soul needed. Indeed with each new day God reminds me of his goodness in both big and small ways.

I have been blessed to meet and talk with some of my blog readers and prayer warriors—people I did not even know. They took time out of their lives to visit me and share how God has ministered to them through my blog. I write this with tears because I'm humbled and amazed. Each of these testimonies have shown me just how good God is, and how He ministers to my exact needs. He sees me.

No matter how hard your circumstances may be, there is always goodness to be found. It's not easy on some days, but it's there. When feeling discouraged, pray and ask God to show you an example of His goodness, and to encourage you in His Word. If you ask, He will do it.

To God be the glory, great things He has done.

HOSPICE: THE WORD I NEVER THOUGHT I'D BE HAPPY TO HEAR

Last week started out as any other week, but the last few days have been a whirlwind for me. As many of you know I have been receiving home health care and palliative care for my chronic bladder infections. However, over time instead of getting better, the infections have gotten progressively worse and the weaker I have become. Being housebound and bed-bound has been a challenge and over the last couple of months I have retained a lot of fluid—so much fluid that it makes it hard for me to move well.

When I visited my urology PA in Charlotte two weeks ago, she did not do anything except keep me on the same plan the infectious disease doctor had me on. Because my bladder situation is so rare and complicated it seems we have reached the point of treating the infections until sadly they cannot be treated anymore. We have gone to other physicians in the state for advice, but Dr. K in Charlotte is the most qualified for my case. Therefore, we have exhausted all other avenues for help unless Dr. K has a better solution in October, but that seems unlikely.

I have great respect for Dr. Love who is my former palliative doctor and now my General Practitioner, and her nurses Debbie and Amy. A long time ago Dr. Love and I had a discussion about Hospice and I told her to be honest and tell me if she ever thought I needed hospice care. She assured me she would, and last Wednesday following a visit from her nurses, they called and told me they thought hospice would be the best plan for me at the moment.

As mentioned earlier, over the last couple of months I have retained a large amount of fluid and have become significantly weaker. Because of this and other reasons, it would be best for me to have nurses visit me a couple times a week to moniter the fluid, the infections, and my pain. Hospice can do this in ways that palliative and home health cannot, and they are able to consult with their physicians and mine to determine what needs to be done for me on a day-to-day basis. They are also able to take regular urine cultures, prescribe meds, and do blood work all at my house, which is very helpful right now. It is our goal that Hospice will help me build up some strength and recuperate. I could be discharged in a couple months or stay on as long as I need them.

Whether it be a few months or years I am so thankful to have their assistance right now. It has been such a blessing. I never thought I would be glad to hear the word "hospice" in regards to me, but even in the short time of receiving their care, they have helped so much. They truly do desire to make the patient comfortable. I am already receiving medicine and supplies from them including a new wheelchair. My sweet nurses Jodie and Jill have been so good to work with and patiently answer all of our questions. So many (myself included), hear the word "hospice" and automatically think of death or end-of-life care. While that can be true, they can also provide respite and recuperation for cases like mine. Realistically my situation could be terminal and could go in that direction at anytime. However, thankfully the antibiotic treatment I'm currently on is working for now and my prayer is that different treatments will help me for a long time to come. Regardless of what I need in the future, I'm thankful to have the specific care from hospice that I have today.

My family and I have been praying for the help that I have needed, and the Lord has so graciously answered those prayers through Hospice. Even though this is the right next step for my health I will miss all my sweet nurses from Healthy at Home. Ya'll have been in my life and home for two years and I will be forever grateful for your care. I love each of you and will greatly miss the joy and the laughter you brought my way on the bad days.

I do not know what my future holds or how much longer I will be on this earth. None of us can ever really know those details but chronic/terminal illness has a way of making you realize what is truly important in life. Lately, I have been reminded of that more than ever and it has brought me closer to Jesus.

My view these days is what I can see from the hospital bed in my room. For the longest time I thought that limited my view, but with open hands and an open heart the Lord has changed my perspective and shown me how to find all the beauty and joy I need from right here. Even in these hard circumstances God has continued to show me His goodness and has challenged me to have courage, wait, and lean on Him. Psalm 27:13-14 says it perfectly: "I would have despaired unless I had believed that I would see the goodness of the Lord in the land of the living. Wait for the Lord; be strong and let your heart take courage; yes, wait for the Lord."

Thanks again for all the prayers. They mean the world to me and encourage me so much. This has been a hard few days because my treatment regimen for pain is being changed. Lots of pain, nausea, and swelling, but until my body is adjusted I will be having more pain than usual. Pray that the doctors and nurses continue to have wisdom to know how to make me comfortable and that I will gain strength each day. While we are thankful for Hospice, it is still sad to know that I need their help. No one wants to need Hospice, so please pray for continued peace for my heart and mind.

IN THE TIME THAT YOU GAVE ME

Over the past few years, I have been reminded that life is incredibly precious. Being sick with a chronic infection that can be terminal changes one's perspective. It makes each moment matter. It makes you live and love that much harder. It makes you cling to Jesus in a deeper way than ever before. Ever since I have been young I have desired to live for Jesus and put Him first above all else. Throughout

~

Life is incredibly precious.

~

life I have experienced the Lord in deep ways, but nothing like I have in these past few months. When it seems like all you have has been stripped away, you can fully focus on Jesus with no distractions. It has made me see Jesus in a different way—really see Him—and in the difficulty of the past couple of weeks that has been such an encouragement to me.

My emotions have been all over the place lately because in the last two weeks I began hospice care in my home, and then was transported to Mercy Hospital for what we thought was a bowel obstruction. While I am thankful for Hospice and the wonderful care they provide, it still makes me sad that I am now a candidate for their services. The hope is that I can be released and won't need them after a few months. I do not know what the future looks like for me, but I will share what I do know.

I have a chronic bladder infection that is not curable due to the nature of my bladder from Cerebral Palsy, but the antibiotics I am taking are keeping it under control for now. The main goal is to keep the infection from going sepsis again and for me to have a better quality of life. Bladder infections can change extremely quickly, so while it may be okay today, I could wake up tomorrow needing to go to the ER. Sadly, we have exhausted a lot of treatment options already and another surgery is not likely.

Also, we know that just like my bladder, I have a lazy bowel which is why I had my colon removed in 2015. Once that got under control, my bladder problems started to worsen and now I'm having issues again with my bowel. I spent almost five days in the hospital last week treating my bowel issues. Thankfully things are working better since the hospital, but there is no easy fix and these flare ups could happen more and more frequently. I am retaining a lot of fluid which is very uncomfortable. I've been on medicine for that, but it is not working as well as we would like it to. I have spasticity from CP and that makes my muscles tight, which is intensified because of the fluid. All of that put together makes walking and moving extremely difficult for me. When I do move, I require lots of help due to my muscular issues and being weak. I have gained so much weight from the fluid and cannot wear a lot of my clothes anymore. As my doctors and parents remind me, this is beyond my control and I'm doing the best I can.

Unfortunately there are no easy fixes for any of it. My infection has been terminal before and unless a miracle happens, it will be terminal again. We just don't know how soon. It could be weeks, months, or years, but that is for God to decide. No matter what doctors say, God is the decision maker and I will not leave earth before it is my time. Life can change in the blink of an eye which makes me desire and pray for those who do not know Jesus as their Savior and Lord. It hurts my heart to think of all the good people in this world who will not go to Heaven when they pass away.

So much joy is missed if you don't know the Lord. The more suffering I experience, the more I can't imagine going through these same trials without God. Without God I think I would have given up long ago and become bitter. Thankfully though, God has carried me through everything.

On a more cheerful note, if you know me well, then you know that I have a deep love for music. For every season I've gone through, I have at least two songs that represent life during that time. When I hear a song where the lyrics could have been taken from my journal, I immediately thank God for that glimmer of hope. Not to sound sappy, but God truly does know the way to my heart. It may be just another simple song to some, but to me it is the encouragement God is giving me that day.

Lately, my music of choice has been Joey and Rory Feek, MercyMe, and Ellie Holcomb. A few months ago a friend texted me a link to MercyMe's "Even If" and said, "You need to listen to this." For whatever reason I did not listen then, but a few days later I remembered and listened. The message hit me in the deepest area of my heart. Similarly during that time, I heard the song "You Love Me Best" by Ellie Holcomb and oh my word it made me cry all kinds of tears! God knows me in the deepest of ways and He does love me best. Nothing can lift one out of the pit better than God showing them evidence that He truly sees them. What a gift it is to be known in that way.

Another one of my favorite tunes right now is from Joey and Rory's album, *Hymns That Are Important To Us*. This is the song that inspired the blogpost for today. While recording the album Joey was battling cancer that took her life soon after the album was released. Her dream before dying was to complete the Hymns album, and every song on it is beautiful. One song in particular that has become a favorite is called "In the Time that you Gave Me." This has become one of my theme songs for this season and for life in general. My favorite verse goes like this:

> *In the time that You gave me, did I face the devil down?*
> *Did I make him turn away every time I stood my ground?*
> *If today is the day You should decide to take me,*

Did I do all I could do in the time that You gave me?[9]

I appreciate this song on a whole new level considering my circumstances. We are not promised tomorrow; that's why it is so important to love Jesus and live well now. No one is perfect, but if we strive to live for Him, God will use us and be glorified. For me that is my only goal and desire—to love Jesus above all else and to serve Him well in the time He gives me.

[9] Rory and Joey Feek. *Hymns That Are Important to Us.* Gaither Music Group, 2016.

REMEMBER CALVARY

Happy Wednesday, friends! Over the past few days I have had some sleepless nights, but each day God is showing me His grace in new ways. One of my favorite missionaries is Amy Carmichael. Amy was a missionary in India for many years. Later in life she dealt with physical illness and suffering that left her homebound. During that time she wrote about things the Lord was teaching her. Last night I read this quote from her that helped put things in perspective for me. She writes:

> Above all there is this, look at Calvary. Look steadfastly. Take time to look and all within you will be hushed. For power streams forth from Calvary. We never need to know defeat.[10]

---

[10] Amy Carmichael. *Edges of His Ways.* (Pennsylvania: CLC Publications, 2009), 82.

Wow! When I read that, it reminded me of what Jesus did for me on the cross. It reminded me that I am not alone in my suffering. There is nothing that I am experiencing that Jesus can't relate to, and He is always by my side, offering His comfort and strength. I do not know what you are facing today, but whether it is good or bad, take time to dwell on Calvary. Take comfort in the healing presence of Jesus. As Jesus said, "In this world you will have trouble, but take heart I have overcome the world" (John 16:33). Praise God for the gift of Jesus! For with Him, we can survive anything that comes our way.

MY BEAUTIFUL TRIBE

I may be biased, but I have the best family in the world! God has blessed me with a truly wonderful tribe! I can honestly say that my parents are my best friends. I am thankful to the Lord every day that He chose them to be mine. They have been there through all the joyful and hard times. Two years ago when my health problems worsened, they helped me move back in with them and have taken care of me ever since. Through many sleepless nights, and so much pain—both physical and emotional—they have been there, never once complaining. Each day they represent Jesus to me, and I will never be able to thank them enough for how they have blessed me over the past 31 years. They are my heroes!

In addition to my parents, my extended family have been amazing as well. You know who you are. Thanks for all the prayers, calls, visits, flowers, treats, and encouragement that you've sent my way lately. I love you all. Special thanks to my sweet Gran who over the past couple of months has visited me every Tuesday and Thursday, and spoils me with a homemade lunch on those days! Love you, Gran, and so thankful for the time we spend together. Also, thanks to my aunt Ellen and my favorite four-year-old Lexi, who visits me every Saturday. My hang out time with my "Mini BFF" brightens my week.

To all of my family, and friends who are like family—I love you more than words can say. Thanks for loving me so well. As Philippians 1:3 says, "I thank my God every time I remember you!" If you haven't done it in a while, why not pause today and thank God for the family He has given you? Don't forget to tell them how grateful you are for them.

LAUGHING AT THE FUTURE

"She laughs without fear of the future" (Proverbs 31:23). Lately this verse is hitting me hard. In 2016 I prayed that 2017 would be a year of healing and restoration. I believe God answered my prayer, but not in the way I imagined. Health-wise, 2017 has been extremely hard for me. And yet the Lord has brought healing in multiple ways.

Yes, I am still sick, and physically I'm worse than I was one year ago. Yes, I am on Hospice and could realistically meet Jesus in Heaven sooner rather than later. Yes, there are many hard days and ugly cries. Yes, most importantly Jesus is bigger than all these things —Jesus is my life.

Jesus holds me and comforts me through the pain. He provides exactly what I need to get through every minute of every day. Jesus knows my life span. He knew the day I would be born, and He knows the day I will die. No matter the circumstances, or how hopeless things may seem, I will not leave this earth one minute before He says it's time. Jesus is completely in control yesterday, today, and forever. No sickness or hard circumstance changes that truth.

Jesus knows my joys and sorrows. Jesus is always near. Jesus will always give me the joy and peace necessary to laugh at the future with each new day. Most days when I wake up, it's impossible for me to laugh in my own strength. But I'm thankful to serve a God who makes the impossible possible. Every morning I have to die to myself and surrender to Him in order to have the attitude I need to survive. Do I fail? Yes, many times, but when I loosen my grip on myself and my desires, my days are much better. My circumstances may not change, but my ability to hope takes a load off my tired body. Surrendering to Jesus helps me live in freedom, not fear. It gives me the ability and the joy to laugh at the future. There is nothing better than that.

HOPE A LITTLE MORE, PART 3

As I lay here in my bed not able to sleep I'm thinking about how crazy things have been. The last week or so has been a whirlwind to say the least. If you have been following my journey you know that I've been sick for the past year but these last few weeks have taken things to a whole new level.

First I was transferred to Hospice care, where my new health team spent time introducing me to the program and adjusting my meds as needed. Unfortunately during this process I began having more pain and nausea, and my fluid retention worsened. This landed me in the ER. After some tests, I was transferred to a doctor in Charlotte, presumably due to a bowel obstruction. Although he concluded that what I really have is a sluggish bowel and chronic ileus. My bowel, bladder, and digestive system have always been lazy due to my Cerebral Palsy. As I get older all these areas have worsened, which is the primary cause of all my medical problems.

In the past few months I have dealt with a lot of fluid retention, but my physicians have been unsure of the cause. However, when the new doctor examined my case he said my fluid was the result of my sluggish system, which made things back up. For the first four days in the hospital, I was on a no fluid/drink regiment. Thankfully, that helped things move along better, and I'm now able to tolerate solids. I'm still experiencing pain and nausea; that is something I will continue to have from time to time. I will forever have G.I. issues and these flare ups could happen more often, but all we can do is manage the symptoms in the best way possible.

I do not expect a cure at this point, but it is very discouraging to hear that nothing can be done except what we have already been doing. This comes from the doctor who is always so optimistic and prone to action.

On a brighter note, God has been giving me little gems of encouragement each day. He continues to remind me that He knows and sees me. One of those occurrences happened last Thursday. In the ambulance being transported from Shelby to Charlotte, I prayed for God to give me an understanding and compassionate nurse— specifically a nurse named Maime, who I knew from previous stays at CMC-Mercy. I knew this prayer request was unlikely because it's a large hospital, and she may not even work there anymore. However, after arriving and being taken to my room, guess who walked in as my nurse?

Maime.

Tears filled my eyes and I immediately sent thanks and praise to Jesus, and told Maime she was an answer to prayer, literally. That was the evidence my heart needed to confirm I was where I was supposed to be, and that God saw and understood me in my circumstances.

During my hospital stay lots of visitors came, which brought encouragement regardless of how I was feeling. Just having some of my close friends and family laughing and talking around me ministered to my soul deeply. I love being around people even though I wasn't able to talk much on certain days, and sometimes fell asleep in the middle of visits! Also, God displayed His love to me yet again through my parents. The entire time I was there, one if not both of them were with me, and one always stayed at night. Their love and sacrifice in caring for me on a daily basis is humbling and I cannot ever thank them enough. Love you mom and dad! Y'all are my favorites and I'm so glad God gave me you as parents.

Having health issues is hard, but God has surrounded me with the right medical staff at the hospital and now at home through my Hospice nurses. I have not known them for long but they have stepped in so gracefully to do what needed to be done. The month of April and the beginning of May have been extra hard because it seemed we had hit a wall, but the Lord carried me through and provided the help I needed and did so in ways I did not expect.

~

No matter how hard life can be, God will give you strength you didn't know you were capable of.

~

I want to encourage you that no matter how hard life can be, God will give you strength you didn't know you were capable of. One of my favorite verses has always been Nehemiah 8:10 which states, "Do not grieve, for the joy of the Lord is your strength." Despite being familiar with this verse, I've often taken its message for granted. But lately God has reminded me that no matter how bad my day may be, or how sick I feel, I have no reason to wallow in grief and despair. Instead of wallowing, we need to surrender each moment to the Lord and He will always give us the strength to face whatever is in front of us. In so doing, His joy shines through us, allowing us to "hope a little more" each day.

LONGING FOR JESUS—A THRILL OF HOPE

I have been waiting for this season for months. It is my favorite time of year. No matter what is going on in life, I am always extra hopeful during the holiday season. Today marks the beginning of Advent, and I look forward to celebrating by focusing my study on the anticipation of Christ. Advent means "coming," as in "Christ is coming." It represents the expectation, anticipation, and preparation for the birth of Jesus. Jesus was born fully God and fully man. Despite being the King of the world, He was born in a lowly manger to identify with us. He came to live and reign in our hearts, so that we may have the hope of eternal life.

His coming fulfills Old Testament prophecies, such as Jeremiah 33:14-16: "'The days are coming,' declares the LORD, 'when I will fulfill the good promise I made to the people of Israel and Judah. In those days and at that time I will make a righteous Branch sprout from David's line; he will do what is just and right in the land. In those days Judah will be saved and Jerusalem will live in safety. This is the name by which it will be called: The LORD Our Righteous Savior.'"

Lately as I dwell upon the hope of Christ, the words to the hymn "O Holy Night" play in my mind. "A thrill of hope, the weary world rejoices…" This year has been a weary one, so it does my soul good to read and study about this blessed hope. I long for Christ and need His hope today more than ever before. I've always been a very hopeful person, but that hope has been challenged as my world has turned upside down from health problems in the past couple of years.

I am Type A by nature, and have always had a plan or something to hope for in the future. However, that has changed— that is, changed in the way the world so often views hope. For example, I no longer have the hope of a job to return to, the hope of continuing education, or the hope of marriage, and the list could go on and on. Even though none of these earthly hopes are present in my life, I have the Heavenly Hope that comes from Jesus. He is enough. He is my Healer, Provider, Husband, Sustainer, and the Lover of my soul.

Jesus is my greatest hope and that will never change, no matter what comes my way. He is the only hope I need. He turns my darkness into light and brings comfort to my weary soul. I am so grateful for this gift of hope, and I pray that you will cling to it no matter what circumstances you find yourself in today.

HOPE A LITTLE MORE IN 2018

"To live is Christ and to die is gain" (Philippians 1:21). It's taken me several days to write this post, but I finally have it completed. I've been in what I call a medical fog, and it has been difficult to say the least. Even though it has been rough, God continues to sustain me. Thankfully, I was able to spend lots of quality time with family during the holidays. Due to my sickness, everyone came to our house so I could be part of the festivities. Those times are the best, and I'm grateful for family and friends who took extra time to be with me. From decorating my room for Christmas to brunches in pajamas and singing my favorite Christmas Carols, I have been surrounded by loved ones continually.

We are now well into January, and the days keep flying by. One of my new year hopes for this past year was for the Lord to provide healing and allow me to be out and about again. My other New Years hope from 2017 was to write more on my blog. While healing didn't come in the way I expected, it is a miracle and part of God's healing when I wake up each morning able to live another day.

In years past I have set goals for the new year, but for this one I am keeping it simple. Being chronically ill and not knowing how things will go from one day to the next has allowed me to simplify my life and declutter all of my plans. Therefore, my theme for 2018 is to "Just live." Over the past couple of years, a lot of my earthly desires, hopes, dreams, and friendships have been stripped away. But in turn the Lord has provided His love, comfort, and strength. I understand what Corrie Ten Boom meant when she said, "You can never learn that Christ is all you need until Christ is all you have."

Those are true words, and they describe my current season of life perfectly. The stripping away process has been hard. It has not been easy losing life as I once knew it, but Jesus provides all I need to live well in the midst of my hard. My utmost desire is to live well in the life God has left for me, and be completely obedient to Him in every circumstance. I have cried out to the Lord for deliverance many times, but whether or not He answers in the way I prefer, my goal should always be the same—to live with the peace and joy of Christ and praise Him in all things.

~

Where there is life, there is hope, and that hope comes from Jesus.

~

The Lord is good and His goodness always prevails. In closing, here is one of my favorite Bible verses, and focusing on this truth helps me get through each day. Psalm 27:13-14 says, "I would have despaired unless I believed I would see the goodness of the Lord in the land of the living. Wait for the Lord; be strong and take heart and wait for the Lord." I look forward to seeing what God does in the year ahead, and I am confident that no matter my situation, I am not without hope. Where there is life, there is hope, and that hope comes from Jesus. He will never fail me. I thank God for each of you (Philippians 1:3).

EPILOGUE

At 4:30am on July 9, 2018, Amelia uttered her last words. She had been silent for a long time, when suddenly she cried out, "Mama, mama, mama, mama!"

Donnie, who was right beside her, panicked and called the nurse. He was afraid she was in pain. But Sara said, "I think she just wanted me to know what she was seeing. She told me everything, and she must have wanted to tell me about this. I'll always believe that."

Donnie held one of Amelia's hands and Sara held the other. They were all alone, just the three of them. "You're fixing to have the wedding you always wanted," Sara whispered into her daughter's ear. "You're going to meet your Bridegroom!"

At 9:50am Amelia scrunched up her face as if she was going to say something, then she squeezed their hands and passed.

"After passing, she looked so peaceful," Sara said. "Before she died, she looked rough. Her mouth was funny, and she couldn't hold her head up because of the shingles. But then after she passed, we cleaned her body, changed her clothes, and laid her back in the bed. And she looked like she was twelve years old again. It was like this beauty just came over her body. People who don't believe in God need to be in the room when a saint dies, because nothing except God could make that beauty. It was the worst night of my life and the best night of my life."

Some of Amelia's most precious friends were her two dogs, Lucy and Coco. Coco is a feist, a small hunting dog similar to a Jack Russell Terrier. When it was time to collect the body, he laid in the hallway and refused to move so they could take her away. Eventually they navigated around him, and he followed the stretcher all the way to the door, knowing Amelia was underneath the sheets. When they shut the door, Sara said he just slumped to the ground. He knew she was gone.

Amelia had requested that in lieu of flowers, memorials be sent to the Vale Veterinary Hospital in honor of Lucy, her cockapoo. Years ago Lucy was rescued from a ditch, and someone donated money to pay for her medical care before Amelia adopted her. Amelia wanted to "pay it forward," and she did. The veterinary hospital was given $3,000 in memorials, and those donations saved the life of a dog who was hit by a car shortly after Amelia's funeral, a dog belonging to a family who didn't have the funds to save him apart from the donation.

Today, the McNeilly's home church, Corinth Baptist Church, offers an Amelia McNeilly Memorial Scholarship. Any college-bound seniors are eligible to apply by writing an essay about how their relationship with the Lord will affect their future career. "We prayed and thought about what sort of fund to create," Sara said. "We considered missions and various outreaches, but in the end we choose to support education because college radically impacted Amelia's life."

While this compilation of Amelia's writing is roughly chronological, it's not exhaustive nor perfectly chronological. That being said, the very last thing Amelia ever wrote was a short, fragmented post to God about the things she's thankful for—small, ordinary things like chewing gum and diet coke. And then these final words: "And thank You so much for my mom, who sacrificed so much for me."

I, too, would be remiss not to pay tribute to Amelia's incredible parents, who are the origin of her legacy. When thinking about children born with CP, Sara wanted to share this message with their parents: "I would never want the hardship of CP for any child. But at the same time, it was beautiful and wonderful. CP was part of the way God made Amelia, and we don't feel bad about that. It's not a bad thing. It's hard, but it made her who she is, and it's made us who we are in a mighty way."

APPENDIX I

More than anything, Amelia wanted all people to know the hope of Jesus Christ. Christians call this message the gospel, which simply means "good news." The gospel can be understood in four simple parts:

God created you and has a wonderful plan for your life. Psalm 139 says He knit you together in your mother's womb. Everything about YOU is intentional, designed by a good God. Jeremiah 29:11 says "'For I know the plans I have for you,' declares the Lord, 'plans to prosper you and not to harm you, plans to give you hope and a future.'"

"What about suffering?" you may wonder. "How come I'm not experiencing God's good plan? **We experience pain and suffering on earth because of sin.** In Genesis 3, when Adam and Eve sinned against God, they ushered the dominion of sin into the world. From that point forward, every person was born broken. Romans 5:12 says, "Therefore, just as sin entered the world through one man, and death through sin, and in this way death came to all people, because all sinned." You and I inherited a sin nature from Adam, just as a baby might inherit an illness from his mother. If you've ever babysat a toddler, you know it doesn't take long for symptoms of our sinfulness to show up! Romans teaches that "all have sinned and fall short of the glory of God" (Romans 3:23) and "the wages of isn is death" (Romans 6:23). In His holiness, God cannot tolerate sin. Imagine if He excused all evil in the world—that would not be just! It would be evil. Proverbs 17:15 says, "Acquitting the guilty and condemning the innocent—the Lord detests them both." Evil must be punished, and the punishment for our sin is death.

But in His great mercy, God paid the penalty for our sin *Himself.* John 3:16 says, "For God so loved the world that he gave his one and only Son, that whoever believes in him shall not perish but have eternal life." God came to earth in human form, as a baby named Jesus. He lived a perfect, sinless life and died on the cross in our place. Jesus took the full penalty for our sin—He received all of God's wrath so that you and I could be forgiven. In His holiness, God required a high price for sin. And in His mercy, He paid the price Himself! Thus, Jesus' death on the cross is a perfect representation of the Justice and Mercy of God.

It's not enough to know these things; we must surrender our lives to God. James 2:19 says even demons believe in God. We must do more than acknowledge God's existence; we must give Him our whole life. There are no "magic words" that will make you a child of God. God is concerned with your heart, not your words. Confess your sinfulness to Him. Acknowledge that you need Him, and invite Him to be King of your life. If your heart is sincere, He will gladly receive you as His own beloved, forever-forgiven child!

If you've made the decision to give your life to Christ, the next step is finding community. Reach out to another Christian, tell them about your decision, and begin looking for a gospel-centered church. We were not made to journey alone!

APPENDIX II

My Granddaughter
A Song by John Donald McNeilly

1st verse
If you could see me with a smile on my face.
My eyes are twinkling at the sight of His grace.
All of the angels showing me this heavenly place.
Heaven can be yours, just keep running the race.

Chorus
Heaven is much sweeter, than what I had thought.
Meeting my Jesus was something that I sought.
Now I am here with all the saints and Grandmaw.
Running the streets of gold, I have no more flaws.

2nd verse
Don't worry about me Mom, I have run my race.
No more pain or sorrow, just amazing grace.
I am shouting victory on heaven's shore.
And living with Jesus for evermore.

3rd verse
Please come and meet me, let me tell you what to do.
Get in your Bible, repent, and be made new.
Bow on your knees and keep praying every day.
You must get ready now and do not delay.

4th verse
If you could see, my new body now.
With all the saints and Jesus gathered round.
Such beautiful scenery could never be found.
Angels are singing with a glorious sound.

ABOUT THE AUTHORS

AMELIA MCNEILLY lived from January 9, 1985 to July 9, 2018. She was an accomplished blogger and booking agent for comedians in Hollywood. In 2018 she received the Alumni Recognition Award posthumously from Columbia International University. Amelia's beloved parents, Donnie and Sara, received the reward on her behalf.

JEANNE HARRISON is the author of *Loving My Lot: A Young Mom's Journey to Contentment* and *Hiding in the Hallway: Anchoring Yourself as an MK*. She lives with her husband, Clint, and their four daughters in Oviedo, Florida, where Clint is a campus pastor at Grace Church.

Made in the USA
Columbia, SC
10 July 2021